NATIONAL GALLERY OF IRELAND

FIFTY VIEWS OF IRELAND

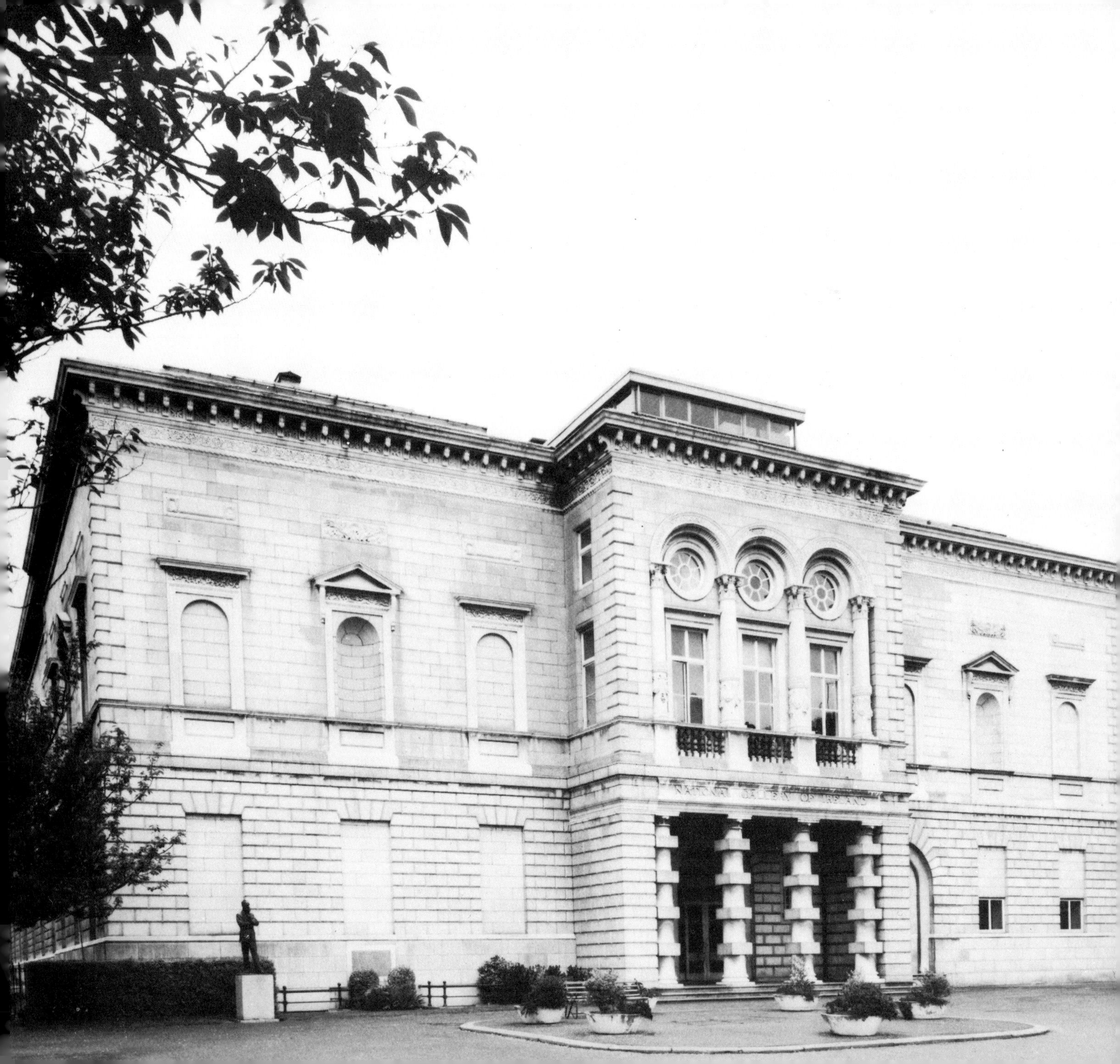

National Gallery of Ireland

Fifty views of Ireland

by Catherine de Courcy and Ann Maher

The National Gallery of Ireland 1985

British Library Cataloguing in Publication Data
Fifty views of Ireland.
1. Landscape painting, Irish—Catalogs
2. Landscape painting—18th century—Ireland —Catalogs 3. Landscape painting—19th century—Ireland—Catalogs 4. Ireland in art—Catalogs
I. De Courcy, Catherine II. Maher, Ann
III. National Gallery of Ireland
758'.1 ND1364.17

ISBN 0-903162-26-1

First published, 1985, by the National Gallery of Ireland,
Merrion Square West, Dublin 2.

Edited by Joanna Mitchel and Karena Morton.
Photography by Declan Emerson.

Design, origination and print production by Printset and Design Ltd., Dublin

Printed in Ireland by McBrinn & Ryan Ltd.

Foreword

In the field of landscape painting, Irish painters of the eighteenth century were outstanding and several artists, including William Ashford, George Barrett and the brothers Thomas Roberts and Thomas Sautelle Roberts painted landscapes that were on a par with those painted by their contemporaries in other European countries. It was from the middle of the eighteenth century that landscape painting developed in Ireland and it developed out of a tradition of topographical painting that went back to the beginning of the century. The painters mentioned above painted real as well as imaginary views and Ashford, Barrett and Thomas Sautelle Roberts are all represented in this book by topographical paintings of Dublin, Powerscourt Waterfall and County Waterford respectively. The topographical artist most associated with Ireland in the eighteenth century is James Malton and the National Gallery of Ireland is fortunate in possessing several of the original watercolours for his famous engraved views of Dublin and a number of these are included among *Fifty Views of Ireland.* In the nineteenth century, perhaps the most important Irish topographical painter was George Petrie. Petrie was an archaeologist, one of the first in Ireland, and he wrote an important work on Irish Round Towers as well as making countless drawings of the countryside which were engraved and used as illustrations to various guidebooks. The National Gallery of Ireland has a number of his watercolours all of which are very fine and of exceptional interest and a number of them are here reproduced. *Fifty Views of Ireland* also includes work by lesser known painters such as Chaigneau, Turner de Lond and Samuel Woolley, and the views represented show scenes in most counties of Ireland.

Many of the paintings have never before been reproduced. They have been selected from our Collection by Catherine de Courcy and Ann Maher who have written about them in an informative and entertaining way. In their text they dwell principally on a description of the scenes portrayed, and in doing so tell us much about the Irish countryside; but they also include some information on the artists themselves and thus provide a potted history of topographical painting in Ireland. *Fifty Views of Ireland* is one of a series of books which focus attention on aspects of the Collection in the National Gallery of Ireland. By means of its lucid text and the colour illustrations which accompany it, I hope it will lead to a more ready appreciation of some less well-known works in the Gallery.

HOMAN POTTERTON
Director, The National Gallery of Ireland

August 1985

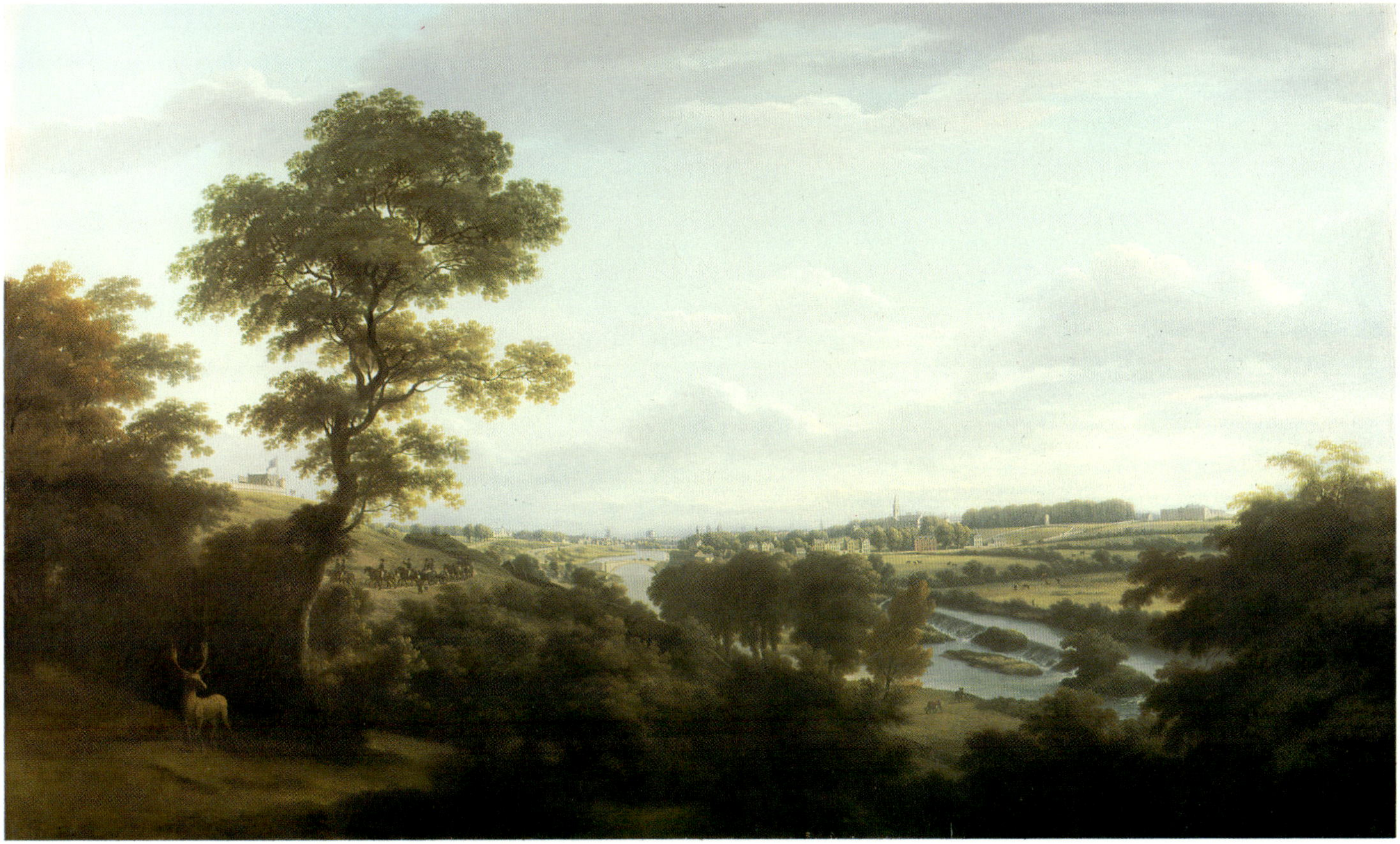

WILLIAM ASHFORD, (c. 1746-1824)

Dublin from Chapelizod.

Oil on canvas, 114 x 183 cms.
Purchased, 1976

William Ashford's view of Dublin from the Phoenix Park is one of two large views now in the National Gallery, commissioned for Earl Camden, Viceroy in Ireland (1795-98). Ashford, one of Ireland's leading landscape artists in the Classical tradition, chose his vantage point on a hill above the historic man-made weir at Islandbridge.

Between the trees on the left of the painting stands the magazine fort. Sometimes known as 'Wharton's folly' it was built in the early 18th century on the instructions of the Duke of Wharton, Lord Lieutenant (1708-1710); he intended to retreat there in apprehension of further disturbances in Dublin following an attack upon King William's statue on College Green. His fears proved groundless however and the partly finished bunker was converted for military use.

Other landmarks on the outskirts of the city include the Royal Military Infirmary, now the Department of Defence, situated to the right of the trees in this view. Spanning the Liffey is the single elliptical arch of the Sarah Bridge; erected in the 1790's it was probably named after Sarah, Countess of Westmorland, wife of the Lord Lieutenant at the time. On the south side of the river is the beautifully situated village of Kilmainham with the Royal Hospital and the extensive gaol both clearly visible in this view.

Dublin City, the focus of the picture, is painted on such a small scale that it requires close examination to distiguish its features. But, aided by the numerous spires and towers including those of St. Michan's, Christ Church, St. Werburgh's and St. Patrick's, as well as the recently constructed dome of the Four Courts, one can get an impression of late 18th century Dublin.

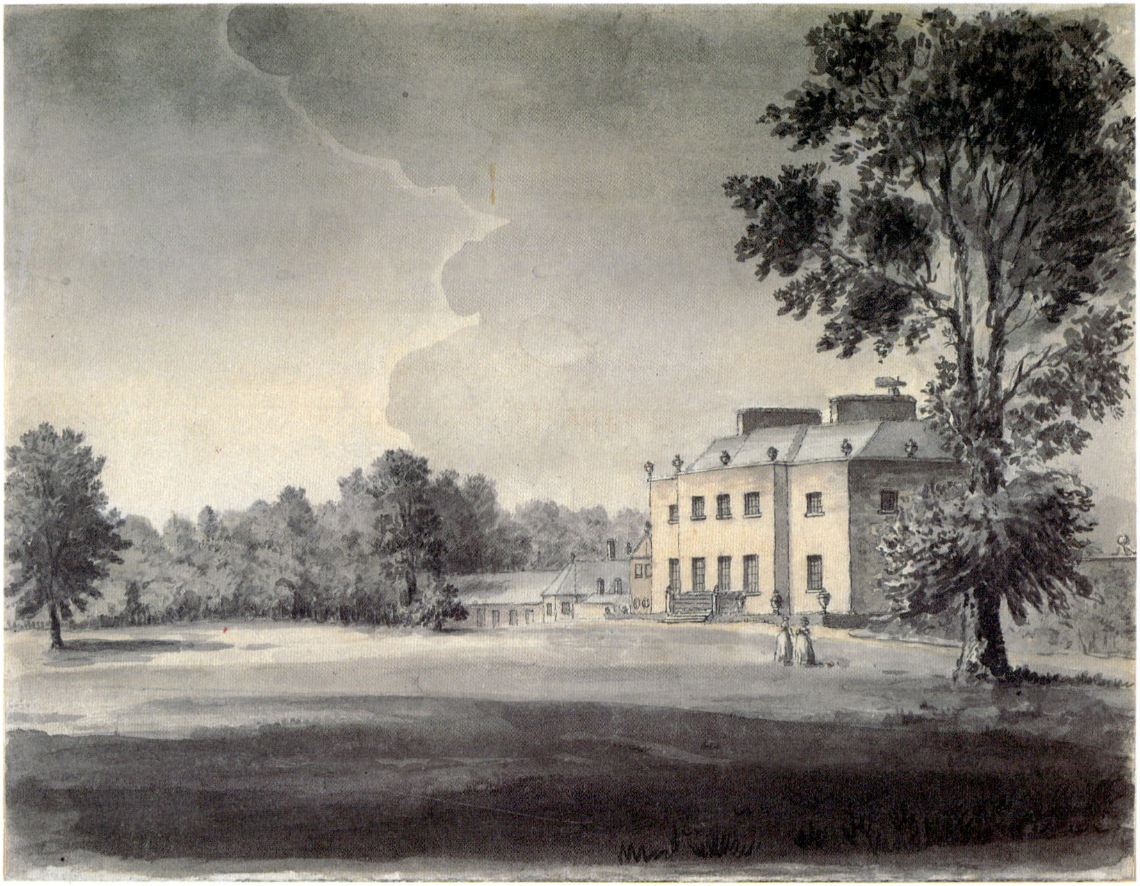

JOHN JAMES BARRALET,
(c. 1747-1815)

The Lord Lieutenant's Residence (now Áras an Uachtaráin) Phoenix Park, Dublin.

Ink, wash and watercolour on paper, 20.6 x 26 cms. Purchased, 1969

Áras an Uachtaráin, or Phoenix Lodge as it was known then, was originally designed and built in 1751-52 by Rt. Hon. Nathaniel Clements M.P. in Phoenix Park, which was at that time the Royal Deerpark of which he was Ranger and Master of the Game. It was sold in 1782 to the Government as a residence for the Lord Lieutenant or Viceroy and was thereafter known as the Viceregal Lodge. After the establishment of the Irish Free State, it became the residence of the Governor General and, since 1937, of the President.

The house has been greatly enlarged over the years, notably in 1815 when Francis Johnston (1760-1829) extended the garden front by five bays on either side and added the front portico with its Ionic columns and in 1849 when a new wing was added for the visit of Queen Victoria. This view was painted before any of the major alterations were made and before the formal gardens were laid out in 1840.

John James Barralet, of French descent and a painter in watercolour and crayon, was born in Dublin c. 1747. In 1770 he went to London where he set up two drawing academies. He emigrated to America in 1795, settling in Philadelphia. He is credited with inventing a ruling machine for the use of engravers and improving the ink used in copperplate printing. Strickland in his *Dictionary of Irish Artists* (1913) says that he was 'an eccentric man, irritable and passionate.' He died in Philadelphia on January 16th 1815.

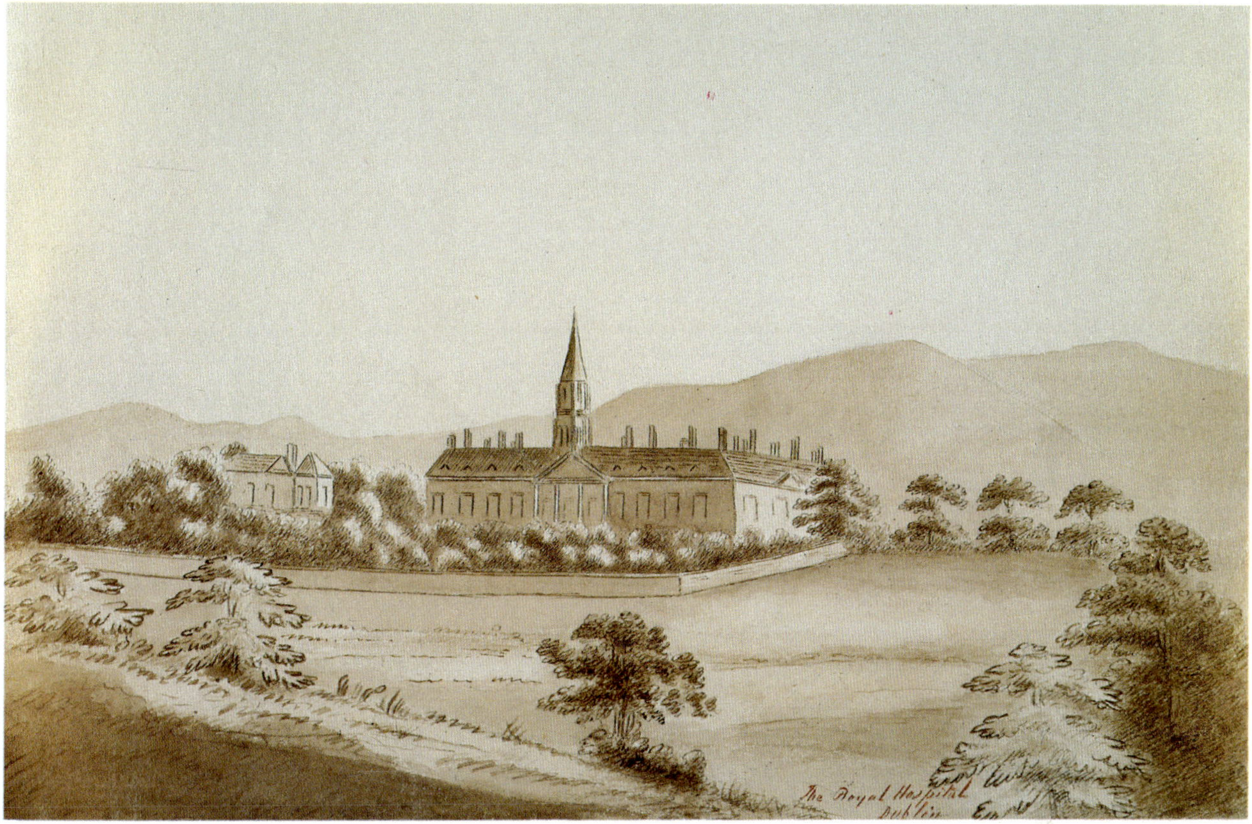

CHRISTOPHER MACHELL,
(1747-1827)

The Royal Hospital, Kilmainham, Dublin.

Ink and wash on paper, 19.5 x 25.3 cms.
Presented, Lady Valda Machell, 1951

The Royal Hospital was founded on the authority of Charles II to provide accommodation for destitute and disabled soldiers. Situated in a commanding position on the south side of the Liffey it was built to solve the growing problem of homeless veterans in the country. L'Hôpital des Invalides in Paris had been established some time previously for that purpose and the Royal Hospital, Chelsea was to be established in 1682. In 1679 the Irish plan got underway to find a suitable alternative to the regular forts and garrison towns for the potentially troublesome body of soldiers.

Construction of the Royal Hospital, began in 1680, and was largely completed in 1684. Designed by William Robinson, it was laid out on a courtyard plan with ground-floor loggia on three sides and partly on the fourth side. The simply designed domestic quarters in the west, south and east ranges could accommodate up to three hundred men. The north range, dominated by a clock-tower and spire, was much more elaborate in detail, holding the Master's quarters, the great hall and the chapel.

The Hospital served its original purpose until 1927; in 1949 it was declared unsafe. Since then some essential structural work was carried out and in 1978 a full scale restoration programme was organised. The Royal Hospital has now been fully restored and will serve a number of public functions. The English topographer, Christopher Machell, made three drawings of the Hospital, and, although none of them show any of the fine external detail, this drawing, executed in about 1800, does indicate the extent of the building and the beauty of its surroundings.

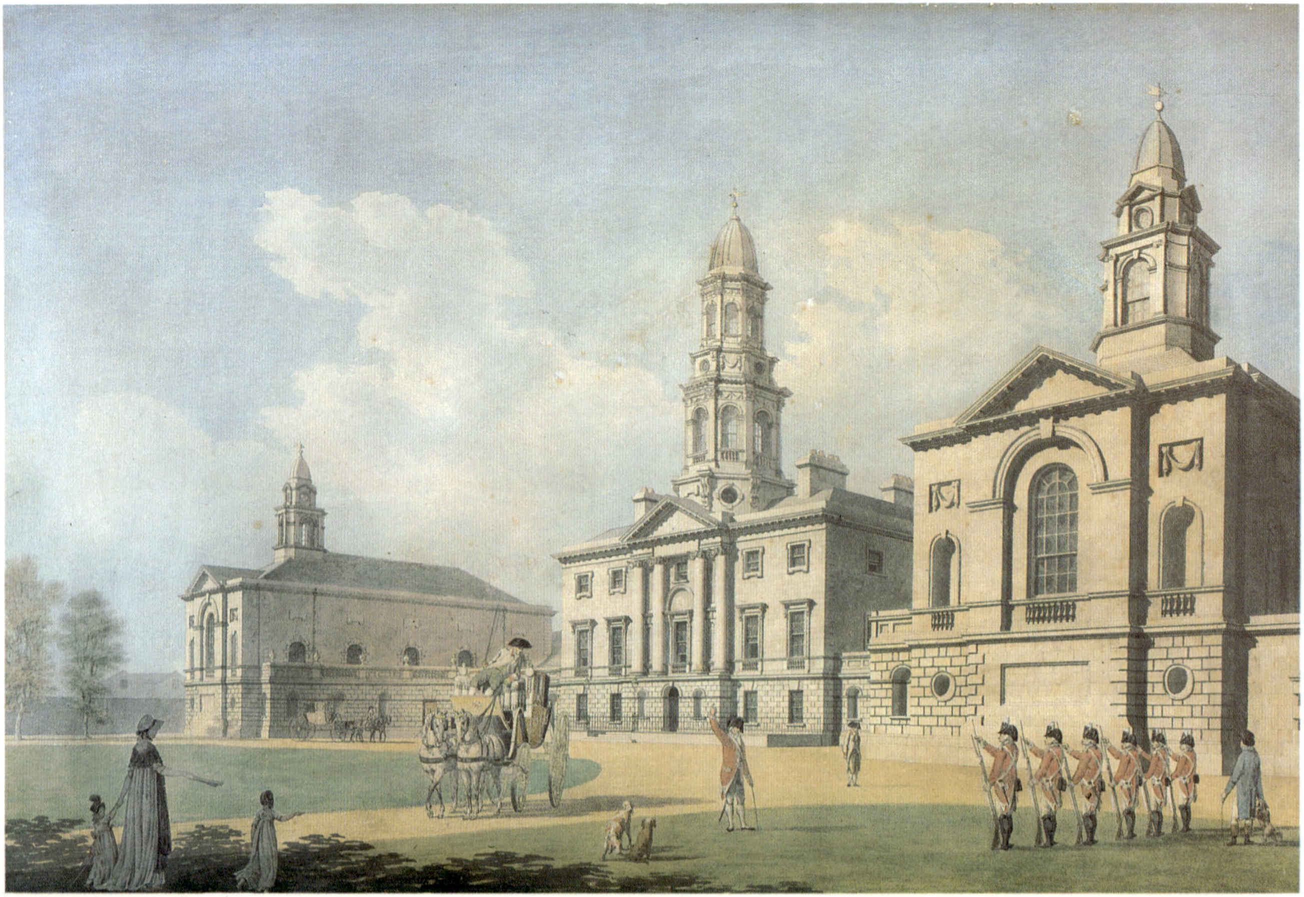

JAMES MALTON, (c. 1760-1803)

The King's Hospital or Blue-Coat School, Blackhall Place, Dublin, as planned.

Ink and watercolour on paper, 52.1 x 74.9 cms.
Purchased, 1914

The Blue-Coat (Blew-Coat) School or King's Hospital in Blackhall Place, Dublin, was built from 1773 onwards to the designs of Thomas Ivory (1720-86). The hospital was founded in 1672 by Charles II for '. . . the sustentation and relief of poor children, aged and impotent people', but was used almost exclusively for the former. The building was never completed because Parliament failed to vote the necessary funds and consequently the cupola depicted above was never built. Ivory resigned in disgust in 1780 and the building was 'completed' by John Wilson. Simon Vierpyl (1725-1810) was in charge of the ornamental carving and stone work. The King's Hospital moved to Palmerstown in 1970 and the building was acquired by the Incorporated Law Society, which promised that all work to adapt the premises would preserve the original character.

James Malton was born in London c.1760 and having come to Ireland with his father Thomas Malton, was employed for three years as a draughtsman in the office of James Gandon during the building of the Custom House. He was apparently dismissed for breaches of confidence and other irregularities. He returned to London in 1791 and died on July 28th 1803 at Norton Street, Marylebone. This is one of a series of watercolours Malton made after publishing *A Picturesque and Descriptive View of the City of Dublin* . . . and is very similar to the plate of the same subject, although larger and with some figure changes.

FLORA MITCHELL, (1890-1973)

St. Michan's, Church Street.

Signed: Flora H. Mitchell.
Ink and watercolour on paper, 41.5 x 35 cms.
Bequeathed by Mrs. R. Jameson, 1974

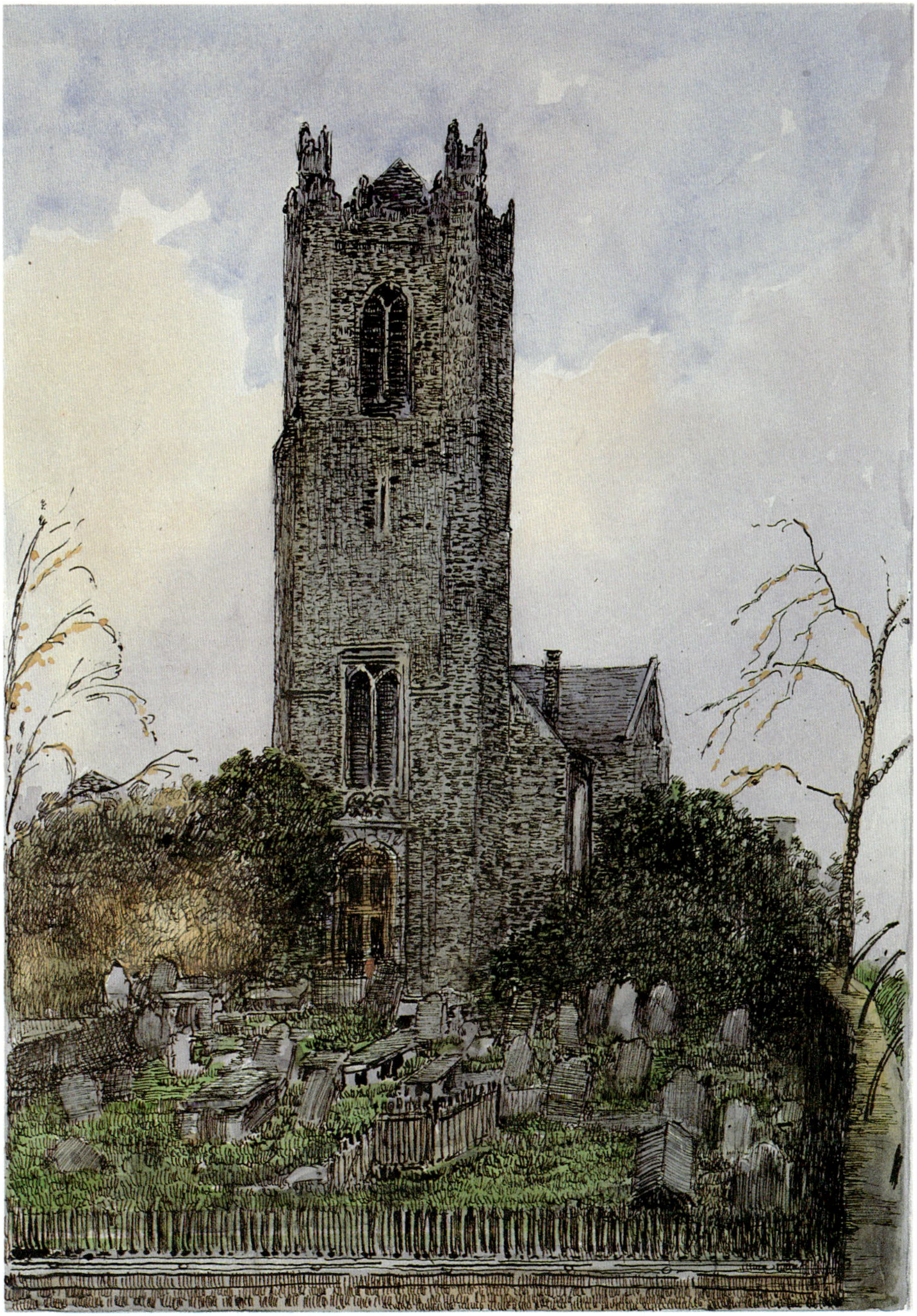

Named after a Danish saint, St. Michan's Dublin was the first suburban church of Norse Dublin and for almost five hundred years the only parish church north of the Liffey. Although the crenellations on the tower give it a medieval air, almost nothing remains of the church founded in 1096. The present building dates from 1685-86 and was heavily restored in the 19th century. Visitors to the vault of the church are able to 'shake hands' with the mummified bodies interred there, traditionally veterans of the Crusades. Actually the vaults date from the 17th century and the corpses are, therefore, of more recent vintage. It is the moisture-absorbing magnesium limestone which preserves the bodies.

Robert Emmet (1764-1827) is reputed to be buried here and Handel (1685-1759) is said to have played the portable organ, the remains of which are in the entrance hall, at the first performance of *The Messiah* in Dublin. There is also a font at which Edmund Burke (1729-1797) is supposed to have been baptised and a Stool of Repentance, the only one of its kind preserved in Dublin.

Flora Mitchell was born on December 23rd 1890 and came to Ireland from her native America only after her marriage. She studied at the Metropolitan School of Art and published in 1966 a volume entitled *Vanishing Dublin*, in which this picture was produced. The plates for the book were destroyed after publication and it has since become a collectors' item. She died on April 13th 1973.

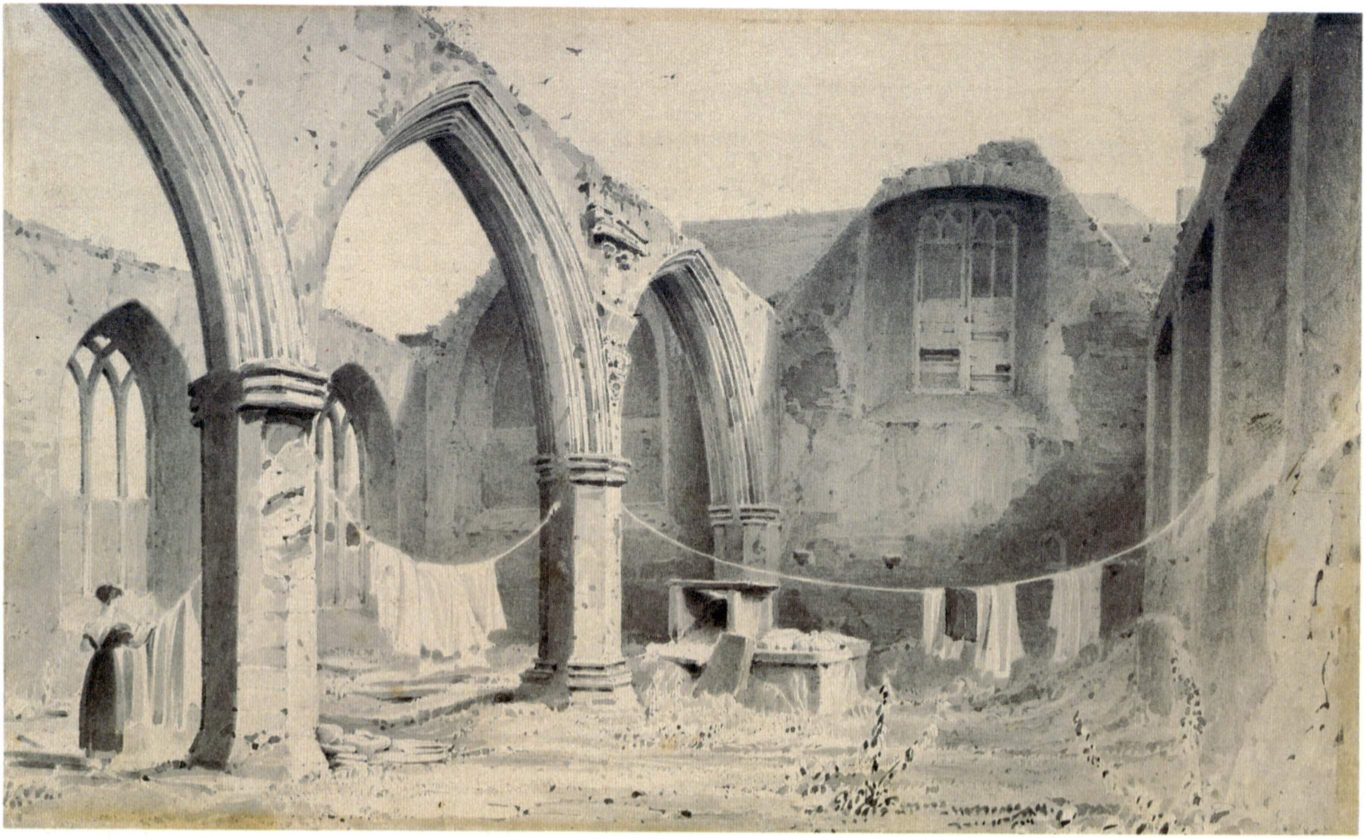

GEORGE PETRIE, (1789-1866)

Hanging Washing in Lord Portlester's Chapel, St. Audeon's, Dublin.

Ink and wash on paper, 14.3 x 23.1 cms.
Transferred from the National Museum, 1966

St. Audeon's Church, High Street, is the only church of Medieval Dublin which retains any resemblance to its original form. Named after the Norman saint, St Ouen, it succeeded the old Norse parish church of St. Columcille. Its tower, probably built in 1670 but extensively restored in 1826, holds three bells made in 1423, reputedly the oldest bells in the country. Two of its chapels, Lord Portlester's, which was also known as the Chapel of the Blessed Virgin Mary, and St. Anne's Chapel, dating to 1431, served the guilds of the butchers and of the bakers respectively. The church is now a protected National Monument.

Lord Portlester's Chapel is the east chapel adjacent to the Church's 14th century chancel. It was built around 1455 by Sir Roland FitzEustace, Chancellor and Treasurer of Ireland. Sir Roland, who became Baron of Portlester, Co. Meath in 1461 on the succession of Edward IV to the throne, was one of the chief Yorkist supporters in the country. Despite numerous charges of treason during his lifetime he died at an advanced age in 1496. A stone monument with a double effigy of FitzEustace as a knight in armour, and his wife, was erected in the chapel. It can just be seen here beyond the washing line but is today in the church porch.

The historic significance of the by now roofless Portlester chapel was probably lost on the woman in the left of the view, who would have regarded it simply as a convenient spot in which to hang her washing. George Petrie, who captured this delightful scene, was one of Ireland's foremost topographers and a keen antiquarian. The drawing was engraved in 1829 and was used in Wright's *Ireland Illustrated,* published in 1831.

FLORA MITCHELL, (1890-1973)

The Brazen Head Hotel, Dublin.

Signed: Flora H. Mitchell.
Ink and watercolour on paper, 46.4 x 35 cms.
Purchased, 1969

The Brazen Head Hotel in Bridge Street, Dublin, is reputedly the oldest public house in Ireland and is a popular drinking spot for Dubliners and tourists alike. The United Irishmen held meetings there and many famous Irish historical and literary figures, including James Joyce, Brendan Behan and Michael Collins spent time there. It is unusual in that no draught beer is available on the premises.

Built in 1668 on the site of an earlier tavern, it was until recently set in a small courtyard at the rear of no. 20 Bridge Street and accessible through a short alleyway. The inn itself was almost invisible from the street. The buildings around it have now been demolished and the Brazen Head is entirely visible, which takes much away from its charm.

Flora Mitchell came to Ireland from her native America only after her marriage. She is renowned for her watercolours of buildings in Dublin, many of which have since been demolished.

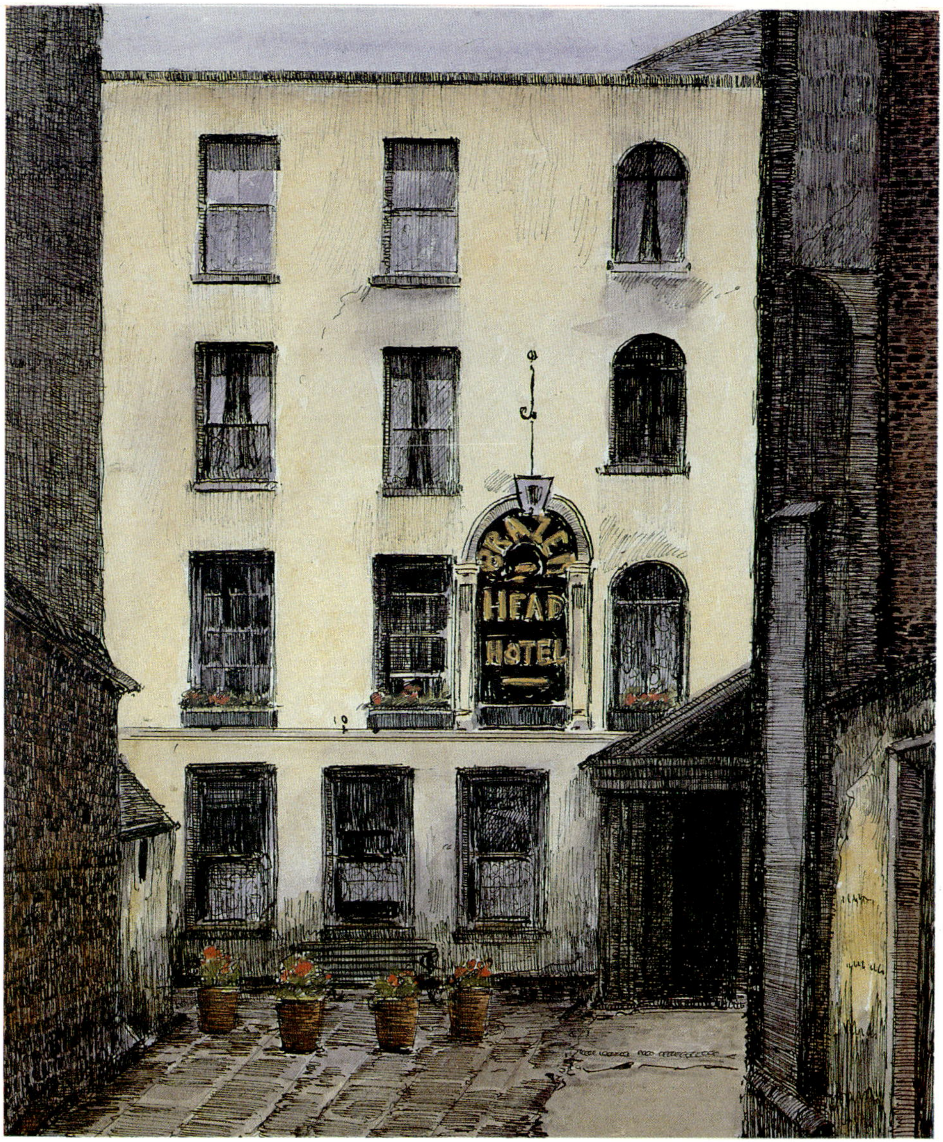

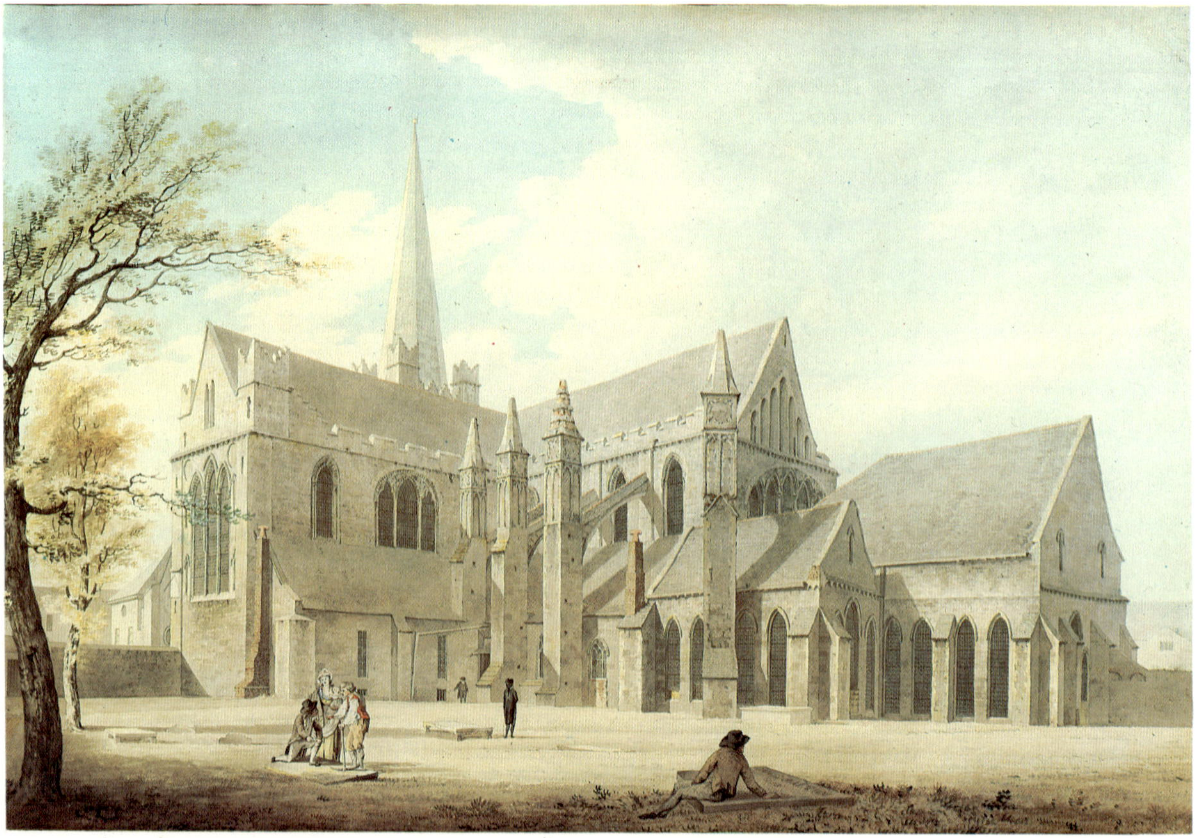

JAMES MALTON, (c. 1760-1803)

St. Patrick's Cathedral, Dublin.

Signed: James Malton 1793.
Ink and watercolour on paper, 52 x 76 cms.
Purchased, 1974

St Patrick's Cathedral was begun in 1191 on the site of an earlier church commemorating the spot where St. Patrick is said to have baptised a number of converts. It became a cathedral in 1213 and was almost completely re-built between 1225 and 1260. The Lady Chapel was added about 1270. In 1362 fire destroyed a tower at the north west end and part of the west nave and this section was rebuilt in 1370. The cathedral decayed so badly over the next five hundred years that it had to be completely restored between 1860 and 1864 at a cost of over £150,000, which was generously provided by Sir Benjamin Lee Guinness (1798-1868). Restoration of the interior was continued by his sons until the end of the last century. This view by Malton depicts the cathedral exterior before that extensive restoration.

In 1560 the first public clock in Dublin was erected on the tower of the cathedral and it is said that Oliver Cromwell used part of the building as a stable for his troops' horses. Jonathan Swift (1667-1745) was Dean of St. Patrick's between 1713 and 1745 and is entombed there.

James Malton, son of Thomas Malton, was born in Marylebone c. 1760. He came to Dublin in 1785 and in 1791 made the series of drawings which he engraved and published in a volume entitled *A Picturesque and Descriptive View of the City of Dublin . . .* This watercolour is almost an exact copy of one of the plates in the book with only minor changes in the figures, which are poorly drawn and thought to be by Malton himself, which is unusual. The artist's signature is on the tombstone in the foreground — a macabre touch.

JAMES MAHONY, (1810-1879)

The Nave of Dublin Castle Chapel, (now the Church of the Most Holy Trinity).

Signed: JM (mono)ahony 1854.
Pencil and watercolour on paper, 81 x 63 cms.
Bequeathed, Capt. G.A. Taylor, 1855

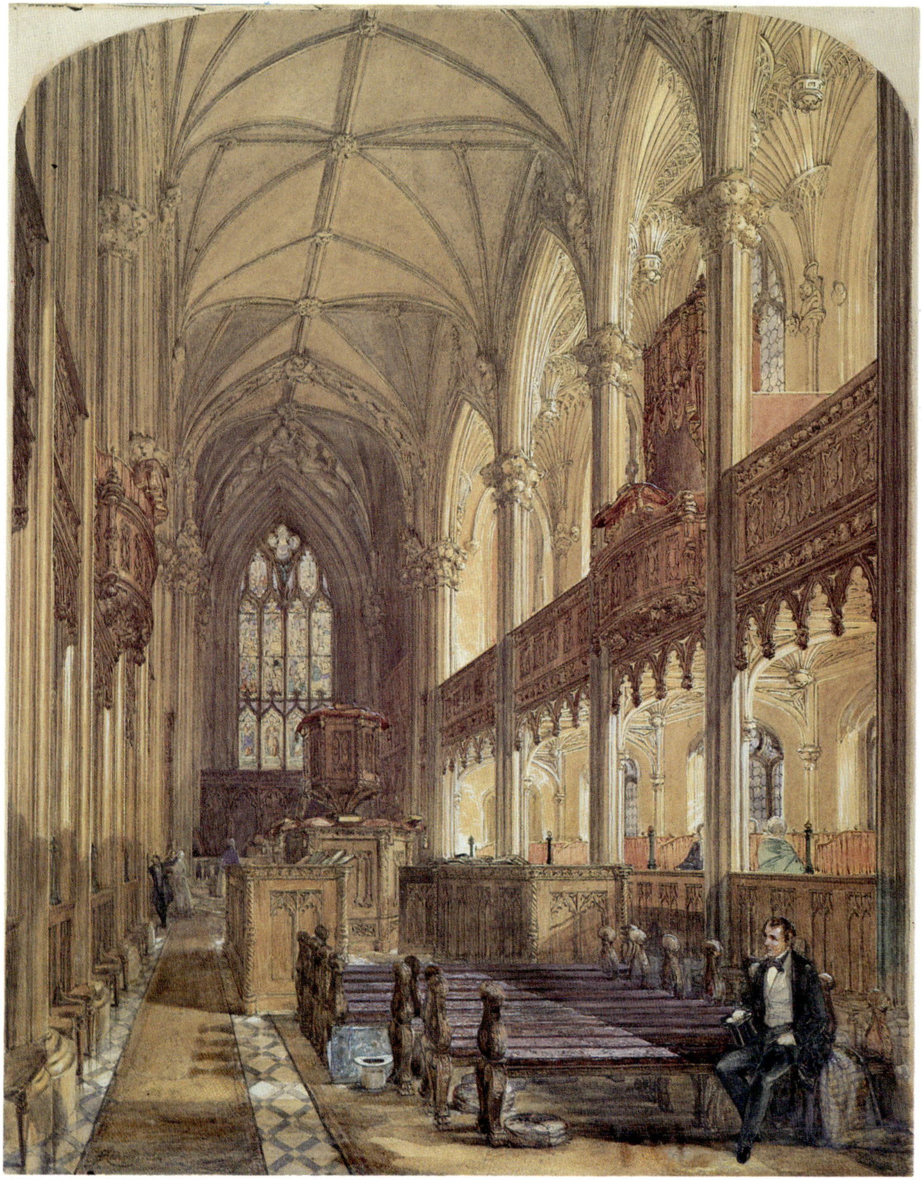

The Chapel Royal was the private chapel attached to the Vice-Regal seat, Dublin Castle. The Castle, a 13th century Anglo-Norman fortress, had undergone extensive restoration during the 18th century; many of the old buildings had been demolished and replaced. Begun in 1807, the Chapel Royal was the final phase of the programme. It was designed in the Gothic style by Francis Johnston, the distinguished Irish architect and a founding member of the Royal Hibernian Academy.

The Chapel is situated in the lower yard of the Castle adjoining the Record Tower. Buttresses, pinnacles and battlements adorn the exterior. The interior, as Mahony's view clearly illustrates, is no less florid. Much of the decor is related to its connection with the Vice-Regal seat. The projecting galleries overlooking the nave were reserved for the Lord Lieutenant and for the Archbishop. The coats of arms of successive Viceroys in Ireland from 1172 are recorded in panels on the galleries and in the windows. Conveniently the last available space was filled with the arms of Lord FitzAlan, the last Lord Lieutenant, in 1922. The great east window, the focus of this view, contains some old continental stained glass which was presented by Lord Whitworth during his Vice-Royality (1813-1817).

The chapel was completed in 1814. The Record Tower, one of the great corner towers of the old castle, was refaced and embattled, also to a design by Johnston. In 1943 the Chapel was reconsecrated as a Roman Catholic church. This large watercolour is one of a number of highly detailed views by Mahony in the National Gallery Collection.

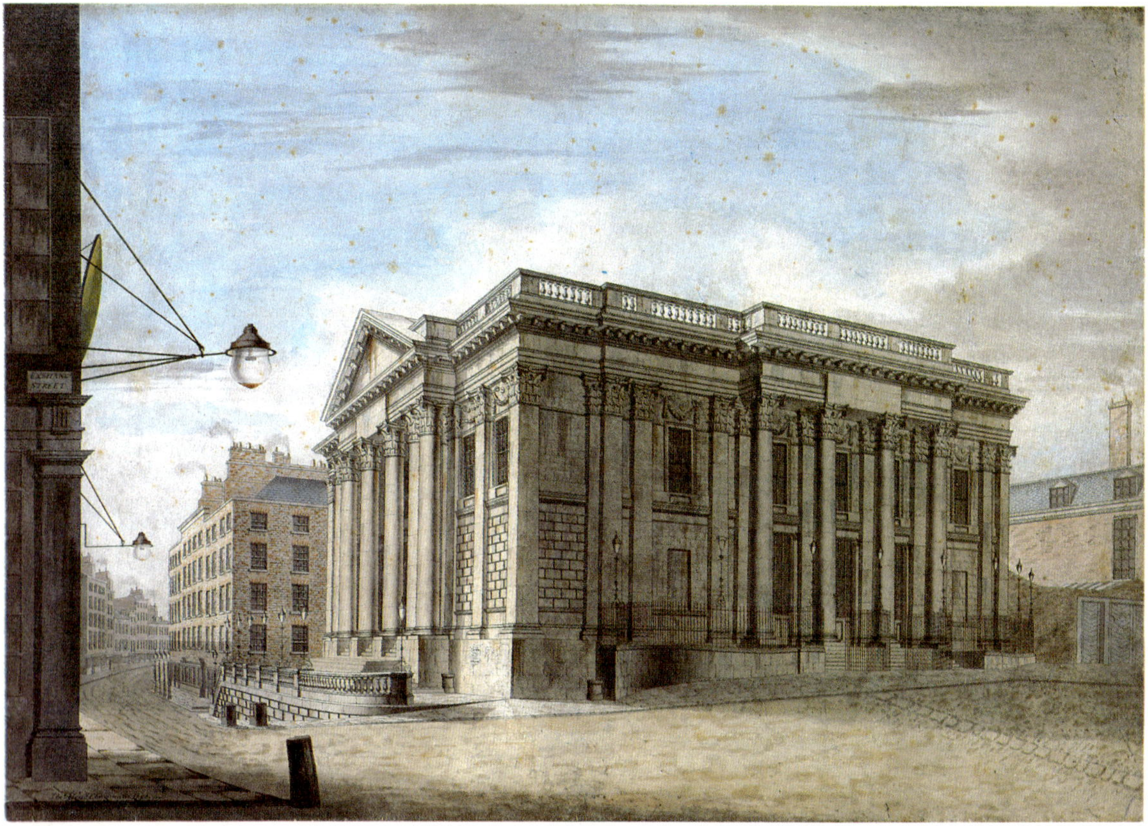

THOMAS HENRY CHAIGNEAU, (c. 1760-1792)

The Royal Exchange, (now City Hall), Dublin, from Exchange Street.

Signed: Tho Hen^{y}. T. Chaigneau 1792.
Watercolour on paper, 42 x 58 cms.
Purchased, 1908

The Royal Exchange, begun in 1769, was built by the city merchants as an alternative to their facilities in the decaying Tholsel. They raised the finance, chose a design by open competition, and purchased a site near Dublin Castle. The site had been occupied by two of Dublin's best known meeting places: Lucas's coffee house and the Eagle Tavern. Both had been demolished by the 'Commissioners for making wide and convenient streets'.

British-born architect, Thomas Cooley, was chosen to design the new Exchange. The site was small but the location afforded grandeur to this solid three-fronted building. The northern elevation, with massive Corinthian columns surmounted by a pediment, forms the culmination point of the long vista incorporating Parliament Street, Capel Street Bridge and Capel Street. The more restrained western front, also visible in this view, is at the entrance to Dublin Castle.

In 1851 ownership of the building was transferred from the Corporation of Merchants to the Lord Mayor, Alderman and Burgesses of Dublin. Renamed City Hall it now holds the Municipal Archive. Standing in the central hall, a finely decorated, spacious rotunda, is a statue of Charles Lucas by Edward Smyth, the work which brought the young sculptor to the attention of James Gandon. Chaigneau's view, painted shortly after the completion of the building, depicts the original railings on the northern front. These collapsed in 1814 and were replaced by a heavy stone balustrade. Little is known of the artist, and this watercolour, dated 1792, is the last known work with which he is associated.

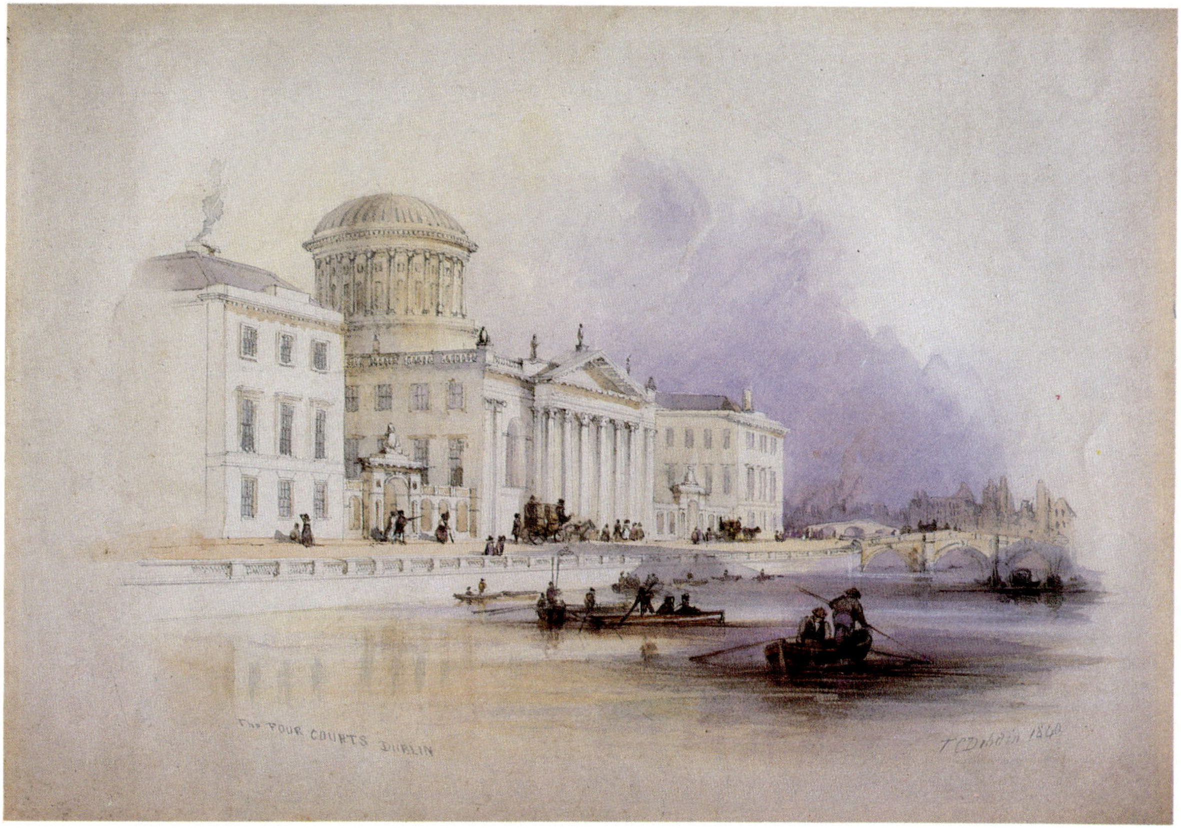

THOMAS COLMAN DIBDIN,
(1810-93)

The Four Courts, Dublin.

Signed: TC Dibdin 1840.
Pencil and watercolour on paper, 24.6 x 34.7 cms.
Purchased, 1924

The huge green dome and the great Corinthian columns of the Four Courts are amongst the best known landmarks of Dublin city. The building, begun in 1786, was designed by James Gandon. The courts were transferred from their decaying quarters near Christ Church in 1796, (but the building was not completed until 1802).

Gandon's task was not easy. The site was small, already holding the Public Record Office designed by Thomas Cooley in 1777; in addition he was obliged to seek grants from Parliament to continue construction at frequent intervals; each time he had to justify costs and each time an objection was raised. Although most of the objections were challenged successfully, lack of funds and constant criticism forced him to make some alterations in the design, the most significant of which was to abandon the plan to set the portico over the footpath.

In 1922 the Four Courts suffered extensive damage during one of the early encounters between the pro- and anti-treaty forces of the Republican Army. Eight allegorical figures between the windows in the inner dome, executed by Edward Smyth, and the double height law library were among the features of the building destroyed. In addition the irreplaceable National Archive in the Public Record Office was entirely destroyed in the blaze.

Thomas Colman Dibdin was an English artist who painted landscapes and town scenes throughout Europe. He exhibited regularly in the British Institution and in the Royal Academy exhibitions. He painted this delicate view of the Four Courts for the vendor's father who intended to have it engraved; however no copies were ever made. It is the only work by Dibdin in the National Gallery Collection.

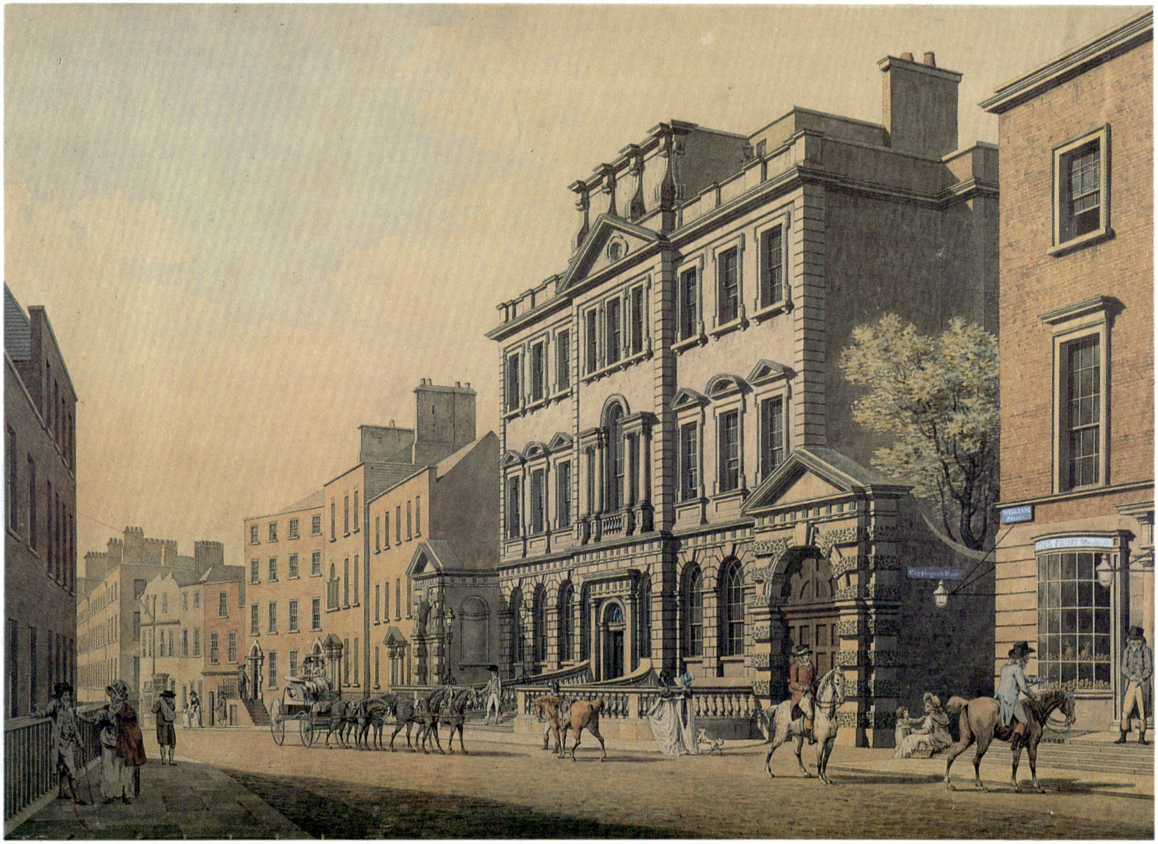

JAMES MALTON, (c. 1760-1803)

Powerscourt House, William Street South, Dublin.

Inscribed and signed on verso: **drawn Nov^{r}.1796 by Ja^{s} Malton.
Ink and watercolour on paper, 49.2 x 64.8 cms.
Purchased, 1948

Powerscourt House was one of a succession of fine, private town houses built in Dublin during the 18th century. Begun in 1771 and completed three years later, it was designed by Robert Mack for Richard Wingfield, 3rd Viscount Powerscourt. Along with Leinster House, Charlemont House, and the Provost's House, it symbolised the growth and development of the capital city during the reign of the Georges. After the Act of Union many of the nobility left the city. Powerscourt House was purchased by the Commissioners of Stamp-duty in 1807.

This impressive mansion, which fronts onto a narrow city street, was built of mountain granite. The gates on each side appear as wings to the house; an entablature of Doric order, which runs along the front of the house, is continued over the gates. Elevated above the rest of the building is a quadrangular structure which may have been intended as an observatory. The ornamentation of the interior is in marked contrast to that of the exterior; the delicate plasterwork, carried out in stages, illustrates the transition from Rococo to Neo-Classical style.

Under the ownership of the Commissioners of Stamp-duty three ranges of buildings were erected around a courtyard behind the house. In 1835 the Commissioners sold the house to Ferrier Pollock, a wholesale draper. In 1982 it was opened as an extensive shopping mall. The awkward angle at which Malton recorded Powerscourt House was in part due to the difficulty of viewing such a large house on a narrow street. This watercolour was based on one of his well known views of the city.

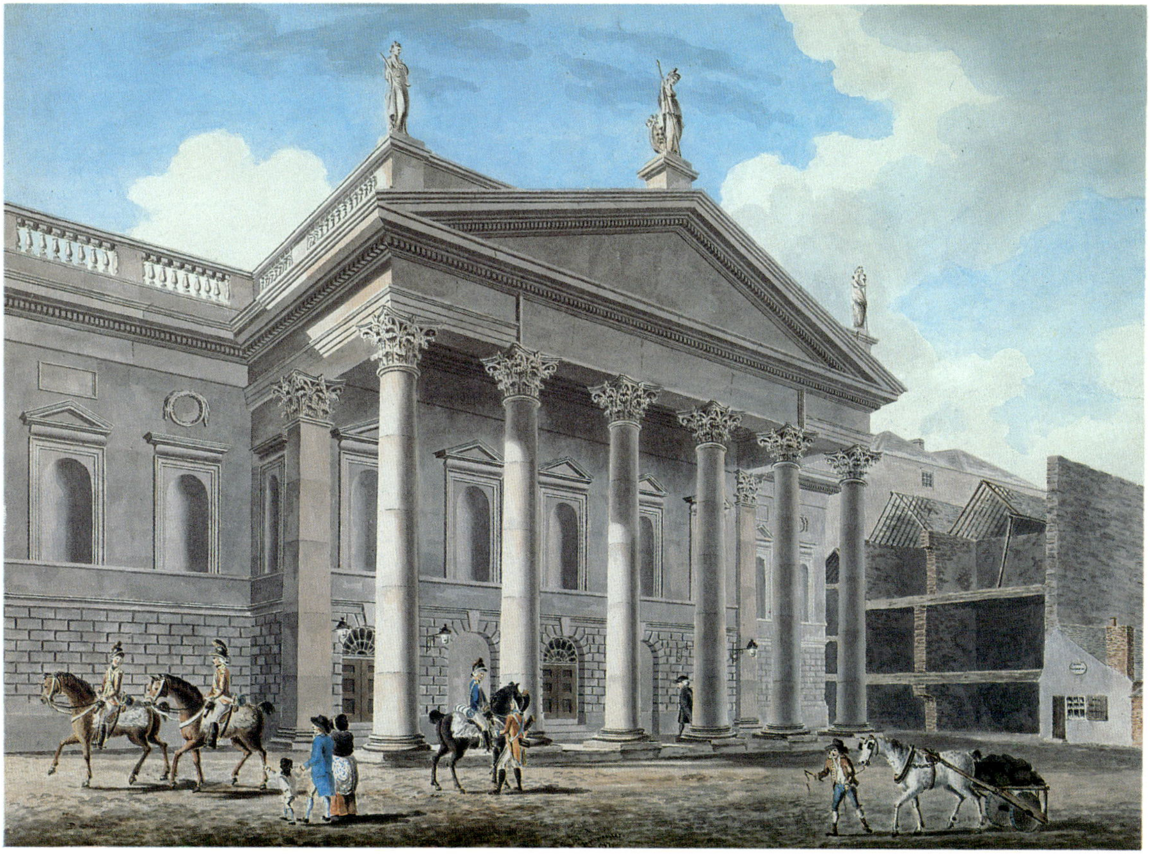

SAMUEL WOOLLEY, (fl. 1791-1802)

The House of Lords' Portico, Dublin.

Signed: SAM. WOOLLEY. 1797.
Watercolour on paper, 40.3 x 53.8 cms.
Purchased, 1912

The Irish Parliament House was built between 1729 and 1739 on the site of a hospital which was erected in the late 16th century on Hoggen Green, now College Green, and used for parliamentary purposes from 1661 onwards. Chichester House, as the building was named after Sir Arthur Chichester (1563-1625) who resided there during his term of office as Lord Deputy of Ireland, was razed to the ground in December 1727 and the foundation stone of the new Parliament House was laid in February 1728. It was designed by Edward Lovett Pearce (1699-1733) and in 1785 the building was extended to provide a separate entrance for the Lords. This extension, which is depicted above, was designed by James Gandon. The figures of Wisdom, Justice and Liberty over the Portico were carved by Edward Smyth.

A plan by a man named Nesbit to heat the chamber of the House of Commons by means of hot air resulted in a fire which totally destroyed the chamber and caused the dome to collapse in February 1792. The last parliamentary session was held there in August 1800 and after the Act of Union in 1801, the premises were sold to the Bank of Ireland with the proviso that both chambers be altered completely so as to preclude 'their being again used upon any contingency whatever as public debating rooms.' Francis Johnston remodelled the building for its new purpose, but fortunately the House of Lords remains. During the Insurrection of 1803, the building was used as a barracks. Little is known about the artist who exhibited architectural drawings at the Royal Academy.

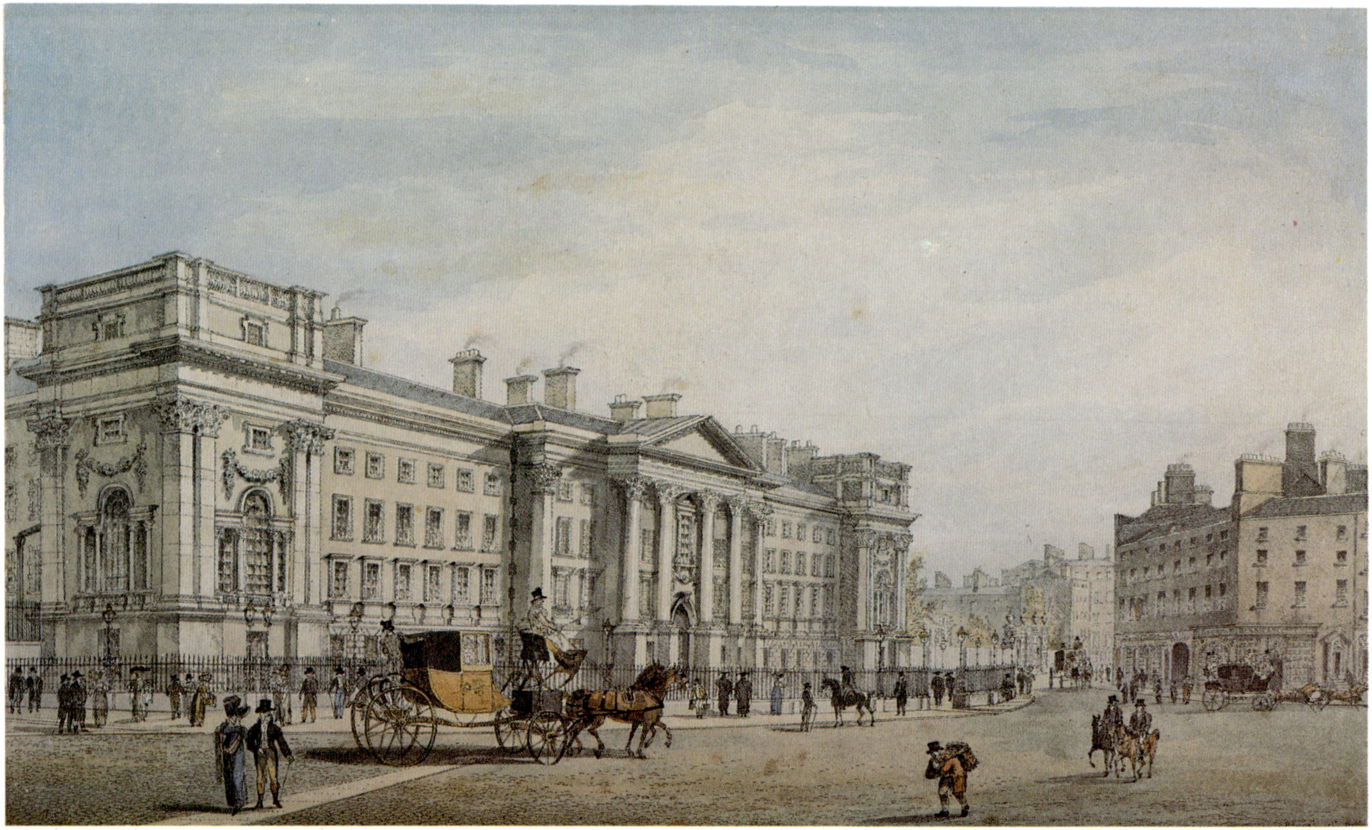

SAMUEL FREDERICK BROCAS, (c.1792-1847)

Trinity College and College Green, Dublin.

Signed and dated:** S. BROCAS del^{t} Dublin 1818.
Ink and watercolour on paper, 24.4 x 40.2 cms.
Purchased, 1904

Trinity College, Dublin, was founded by Queen Elizabeth I on the site of the Augustinian Priory of All Hallows in 1592. The Palladian facade of the west front (shown above), which faces College Green (known formerly as Hoggen Green) was until recently attributed to Henry Keane (1726-1776) and John Sanderson (d.1783) of London and was built between 1752 and 1759. It is now thought to be the work of Theodore Jacobsen (d.1772) a gentleman architect, who designed the Foundling Hospital in London. The stone carving was carried out by David Sheehan (d.1756).

The College complex is now cruciform in plan with Library Square in the centre, Front (or Parliament) square to the west, 'Botany Bay' to the north, New Square to the east and Fellows' Square to the south. Fellows' Square was only completed with the recent erection of the new Arts and Social Sciences' building which opens onto Nassau Street. To the right of this view, but hidden from sight, is the Provost's House which was built in the early 1760s and is the only Georgian House in Dublin still serving its original purpose. In July 1984 the roof and upper floor of the Dining Hall in Front Square, designed by Richard Cassels, were destroyed by fire.

Samuel Frederick Brocas, second son of Henry Brocas, was born c.1792. He was a landscape painter in both oils and watercolour and he exhibited at the Royal Hibernian Academy between 1828 and 1847. This painting of Trinity College is very similar to that by James Malton, which is also in the National Gallery of Ireland.

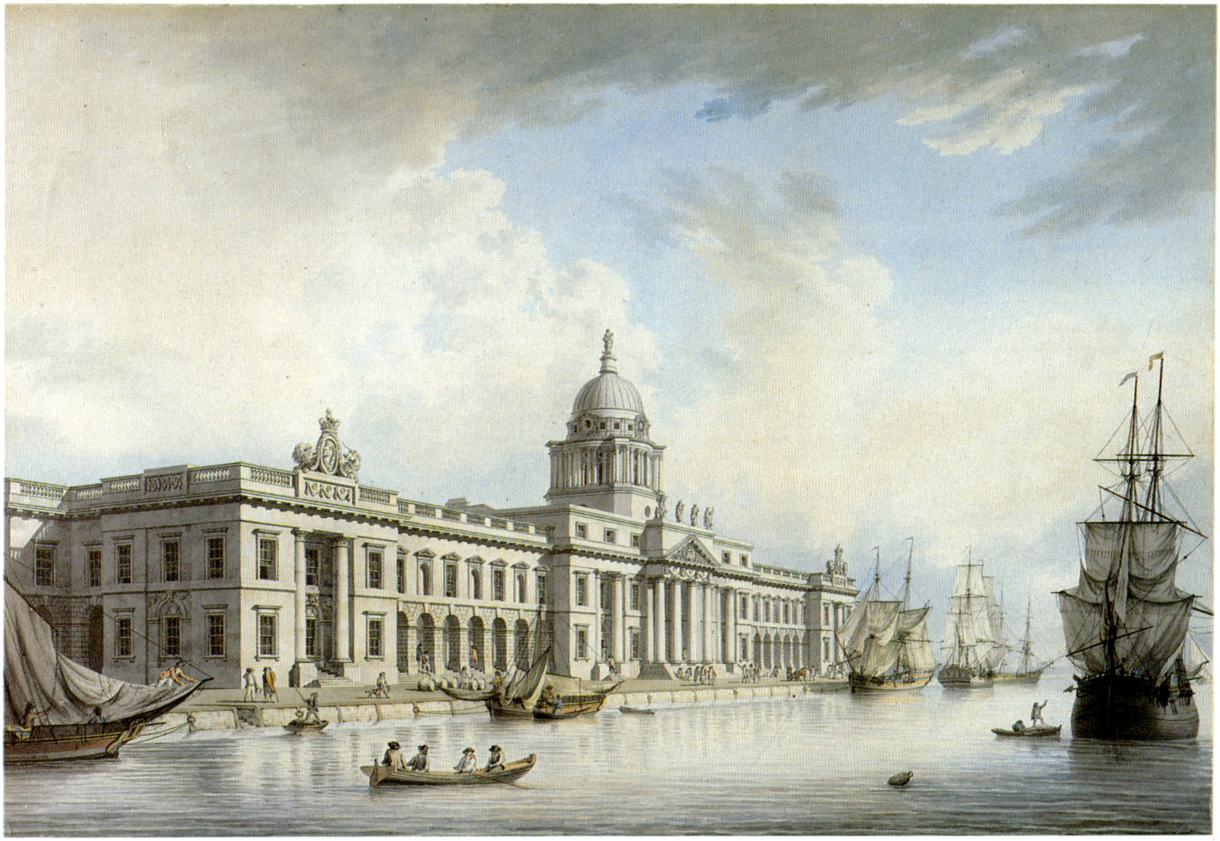

JAMES MALTON, (c.1760-1803)

The Custom House, Dublin.

Signed: James Malton del. 1793.
Ink and watercolour on paper, 53.6 x 77 cms.
Purchased, 1914.

The Custom House on the north bank of the Liffey was the first of James Gandon's contributions to the development of Georgian Dublin. Opened in 1791, it replaced the old Custom House of Essex Quay. The city merchants were greatly opposed to the transfer of an essential aspect of their business life down-river but John Beresford, then Chief Commissioner for the Irish Revenue, was determined to procede with the plan. Beresford persuaded London-based architect, James Gandon, to design the new building. However when Gandon arrived in Dublin, the controversy was such that he was unable to examine the site or, indeed, to visit his friends. When he did get the opportunity to walk over the proposed site he expressed alarm: it was reclaimed slob land near the mouth of the river, a portion of which was inundated at spring tide. His difficulties were compounded by legal complications pertaining to the title of the land.

Nevertheless the first stone was laid in 1781 by Beresford, albeit without any ceremony. Construction was disrupted firstly by the Dublin mob encouraged by the city merchants. It was later disrupted by union problems among his Irish and British labourers. However Gandon was pleasantly surprised by the dedication and skill of some of his Irish craftsmen. Foremost amongst them was Edward Smyth who executed a great deal of decorative stonework. The Custom House was partially destroyed by fire in 1921. It was later rebuilt with some major alterations. Malton's view was one of those based on his renowned set of prints.

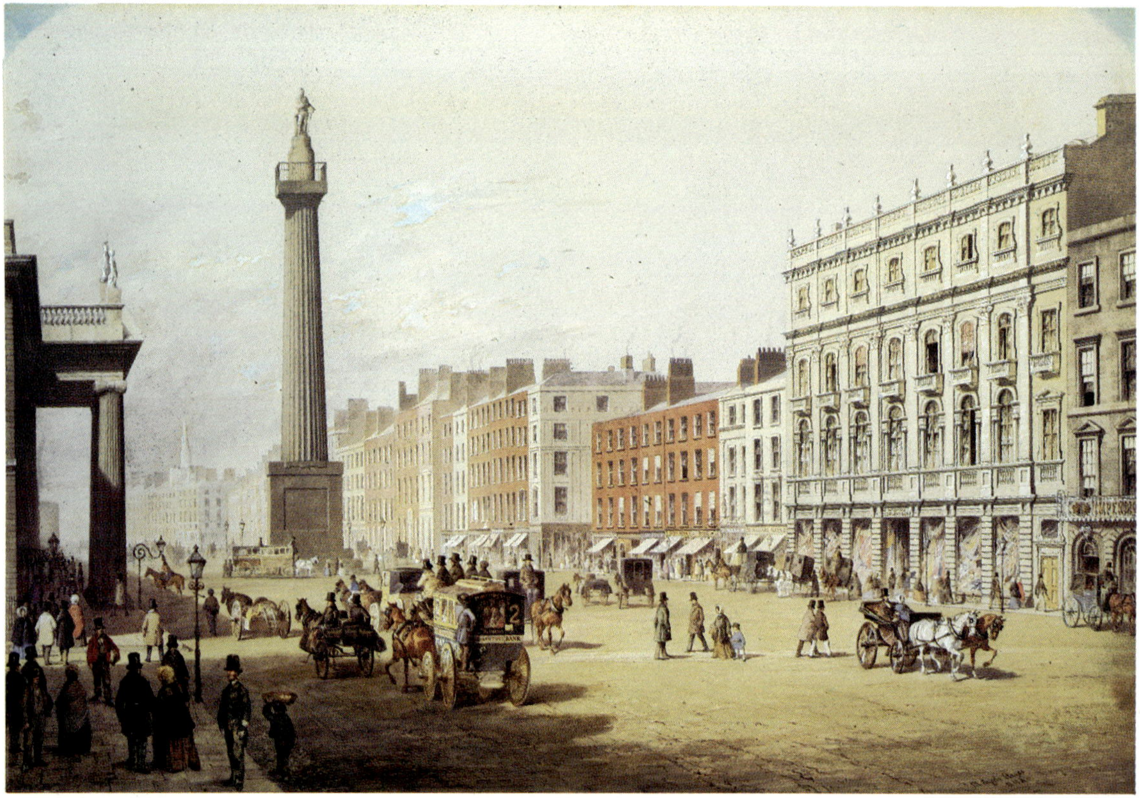

MICHAEL ANGELO HAYES,
(1820-1877)

Sackville Street, Dublin.

Signed: M Angelo Hayes R H A.

Watercolour with white highlight on paper,
54.5 x 77.6 cms.
Purchased, 1942

O'Connell Street in Dublin City has been known as both Drogheda and Sackville Street; Drogheda Street after the Earl of Drogheda from whom Luke Gardiner (d.1755) acquired the land in 1714 and Sackville Street after Lionel Cranfield Sackville, Lord Lieutenant of Ireland (1731-17 and 1751-55). It takes its present name from 'The Liberator' Daniel O'Connell (1775-1847). The width of the street is due to the work of Luke Gardiner.

To the left of the picture can be seen the portico of the General Post Office (1814-18) designed by Francis Johnston, damaged by gunfire in 1916 and rebuilt by the Office of Public Works in 1929. The Proclamation of Independence was read out by Patrick Pearse in front of the General Post Office. In the centre is Nelson Pillar, a famous landmark which was partially destroyed by an explosion on March 7th 1966 and demolished by Army engineers two days later. The foundation stone of the pillar was laid on February 15th 1808 and it cost £6,857 to build. The column was one hundred and thirty four feet high with a thirteen foot statue of Admiral Nelson in Portland stone on top carved by Thomas Kirk (1781-1845), who also was responsible for the statues of Hibernia, Mercury and Fidelity over the General Post Office. The large building on the right is the Imperial Hotel, bought in 1902 by Clery & Co. and demolished to make room for the present store in the 1920s.

Michael Angelo Hayes, son of Edward Hayes the portraitist, was born on July 25th 1820 in Waterford. He was a horse painter who specialised in military subjects, but he did paint a number of topographical views. He was appointed Military Painter-in-Ordinary to the Lord Lieutenant in 1842. While examining a tank at the top of his house, No. 4 Salem Place, on December 31st 1877, he fell in and was drowned. He is buried in Glasnevin Cemetery.

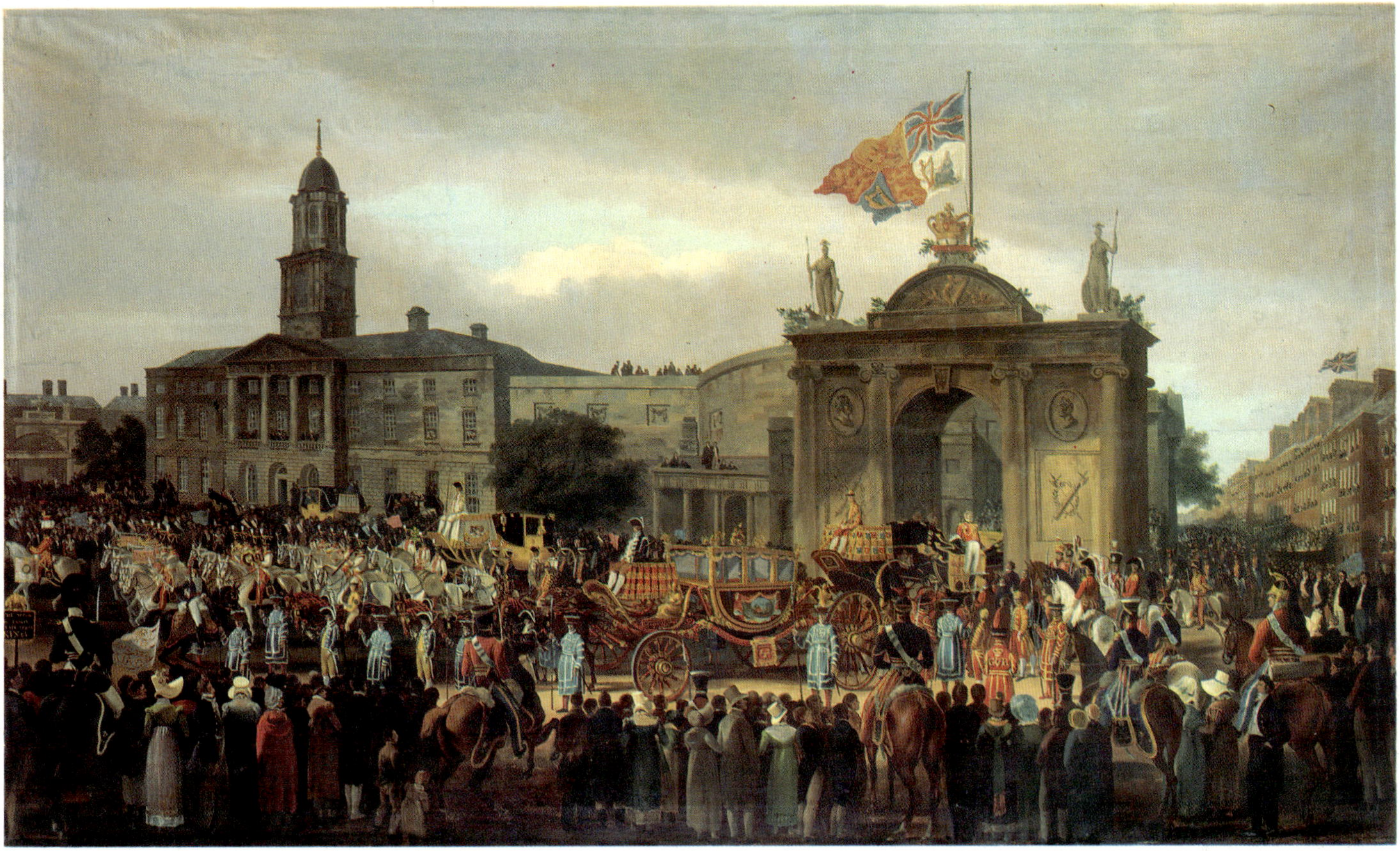

WILLIAM TURNER DE LOND, (fl. 1767-1827)

George IV, King of England, Entering Dublin, 1821.

Oil on canvas, 171 x 279 cms.
Presented, Friends of the National Collections of Ireland, 1947

The Rotunda Hospital in Dublin, seen here behind the King's procession, was originally called the 'Hospital for Poor Lying-in-Women'. It was first opened in 1745 in a large house in George's Lane, now South Great George's Street, by Dr. Bartholomew Mosse (1712-1759) and was the first maternity hospital in either Great Britain or Ireland. It moved to its present building, designed by Richard Cassels (c.1690-1751) and executed after his death by his pupil John Ensor (fl. 1750-1770), in the years 1751 to 1757.

The Rotunda, from which the hospital now derives its name, was built in 1764 by John Ensor and improved by James Gandon (1743-1823) in 1786. The frieze and coade stone plaques are by Edward Smyth (1749-1812). The Rotunda (then an assembly room and now a cinema) and the gardens at the rear of the hospital (then a pleasure ground and now the site of the Nurses' Home) were part of the hospital complex and built for revenue-raising purposes.

This view of the hospital was painted during the visit to Ireland of King George IV between August 12th and September 3rd 1821 and the Grand Arch which was built in his honour, partially obscures the Rotunda. There was heated debate as to whether William Turner and Joseph Mallord William Turner R.A. (1775-1851) were the same person in the *Connoisseur* of 1906 and it is not known if the addition of 'de Lond' to his name was meant to cause or to prevent this kind of confusion.

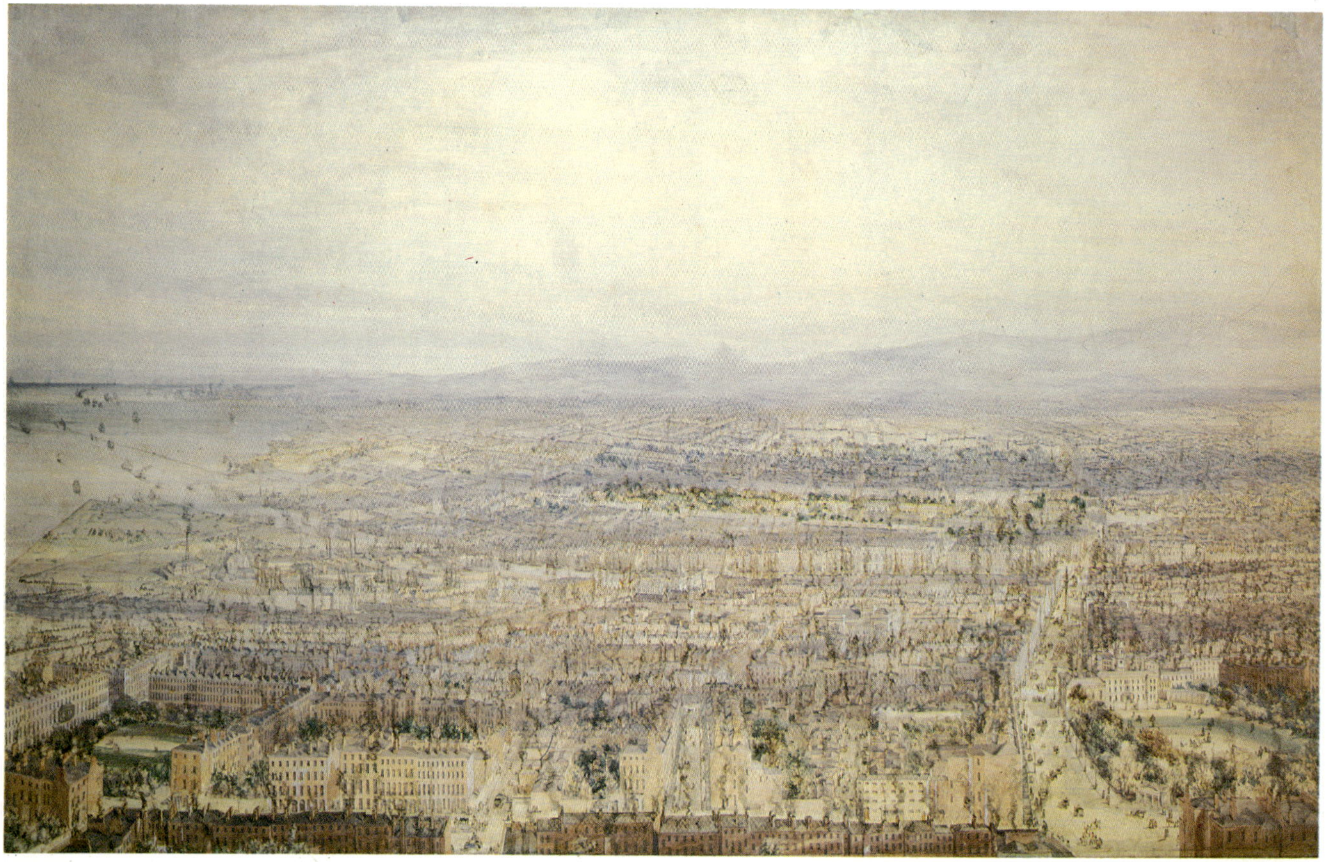

JAMES MAHONY, (1810-1879)

Dublin from the Spire of St. George's, Hardwicke Place.

Signed: James Mahony. 1854.
Ink and watercolour on paper, 105 x 164.7 cms.
Bequeathed by Capt. G.A. Taylor, 1855

Mahony sketched his huge watercolour view of Dublin while sitting in the spire of St. George's Church, Hardwicke Place. The two hundred foot spire of the early 19th century church was situated in what was then the modern part of Dublin and was thus an excellent vantage point from which to record the city.

The north city squares are clearly delineated in the foreground of the picture: Rutland Square (now Parnell Sq.) on the right was completed in the 1770s and was the earliest of its type in Dublin; Mountjoy Square, named after Luke Gardiner, Lord Mountjoy, is on the left; North Great George's Street, Temple Street — a continuation of Hardwicke Place — and Gardiner Street are the three major streets between them. Most of the area was developed in the 18th and 19th centuries when it was part of the Gardiner Estate. As the fashionable area of Dublin it was rivalled only by the Fitzwilliam, or Pembroke, Estate on the south side of the Liffey. Although Mahony's perspective of the Fitzwilliam Streets is not perfect in this view the elegant layout of the area is apparent. The massive temporary hall built for the 1853 Industrial Exhibition can be seen standing on the site in Merrion Square which was to become the location of the National Gallery shortly afterwards.

Such is the clarity of Mahony's view that many more of the city's contemporary landmarks can be identified. Born in Cork, Mahony worked in Dublin for a period before leaving Ireland in 1859 to settle in London where he died in 1879.

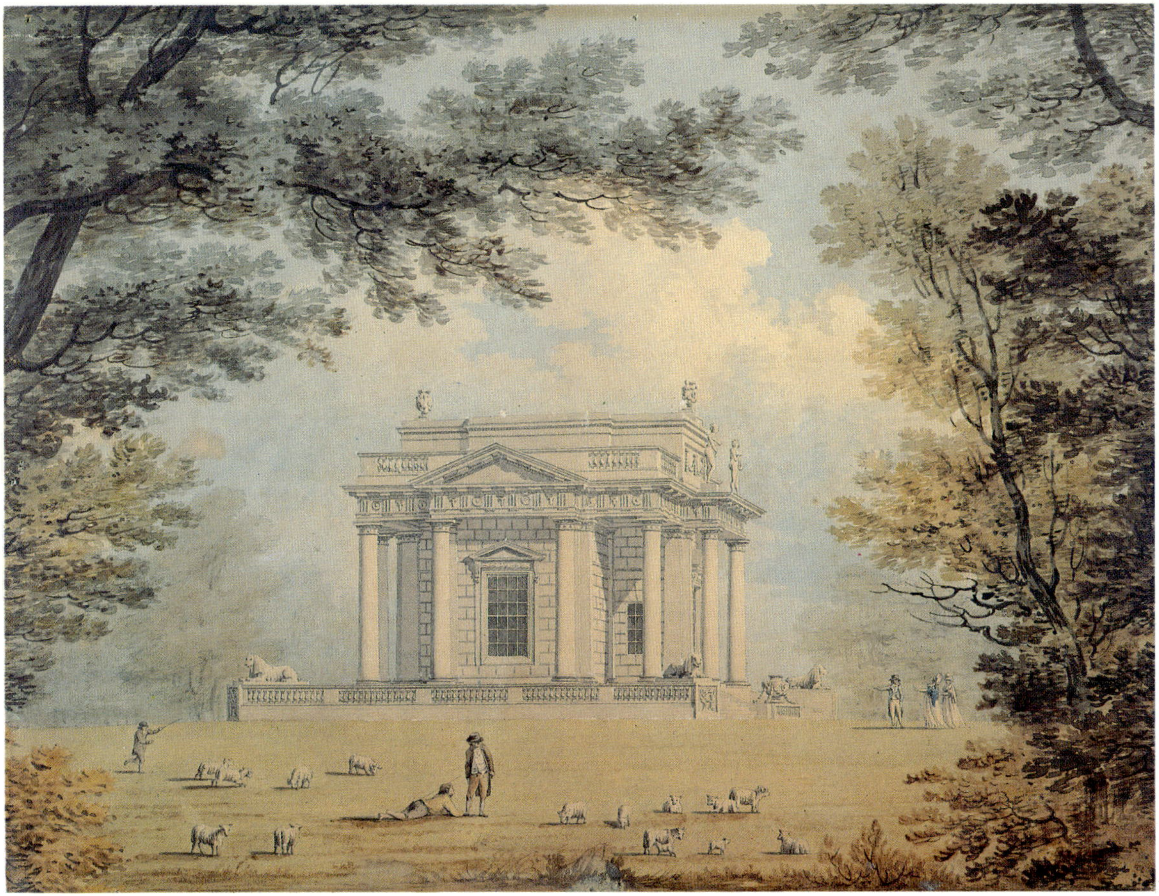

JAMES MALTON, (c.1760-1803)

Lord Charlemont's Casino at Marino, Dublin, from the West.

Inscribed and signed on verso:** drawn March 1795 by James Malton.**
Ink and watercolour on paper, 30.5 x 39.5 cms.
Purchased, 1912

Marino Casino was erected between 1758 and 1771 by Simon Vierpyl (1725-1810) in the grounds of the country house of James Caulfield, 1st Earl of Charlemont at Clontarf, Dublin. It was designed by Sir William Chambers (1723-1796) who was also responsible for Lord Charlemont's town house in Parnell Square, now the Hugh Lane Municipal Gallery of Modern Art. Edward Smyth (1749-1812), who was an apprentice of Vierpyl's at the time, may have assisted with the sculpture. The four guardian lions were carved by Joseph Wilton. Built in the form of a Roman Doric Temple, the Casino appears to be a single storey building but it has, in fact, three storeys and sixteen rooms.

The Casino is considered to be one of the gems of 18th century architecture in Britain or Ireland and is reputed to have cost £60,000. It is the only National Monument post-dating 1700. Restoration, begun in 1975 during European Architectural Heritage Year, has only recently been completed and the Casino opened to the public after years of neglect.

James Malton is famed for the series of drawings of Dublin which he completed in 1791 and which he etched and began to publish in London the following year. Born c.1760, there are conflicting claims about the manner of his death. Some say that he died of a brain fever on July 28th 1803, others that he took his own life in Marylebone Fields.

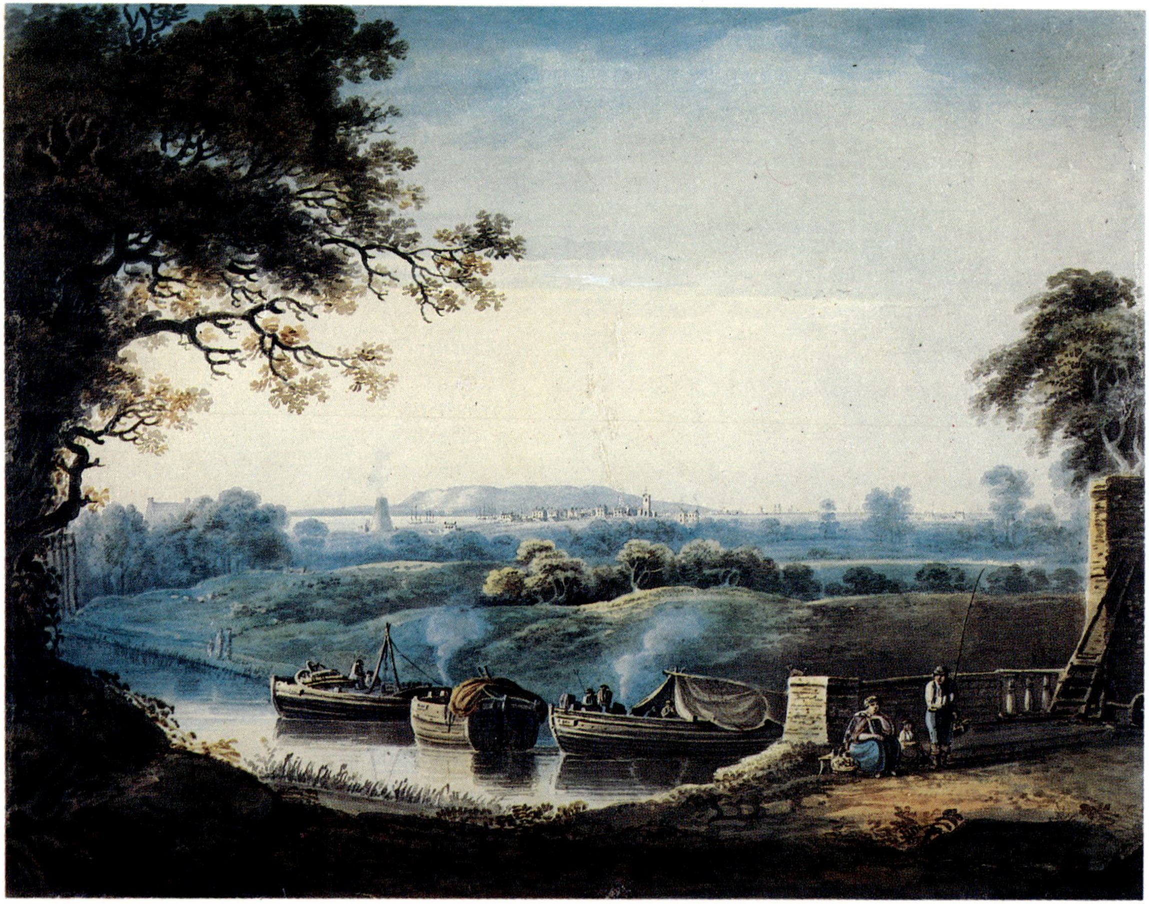

JOHN HENRY CAMPBELL,
(c. 1755-1828)

Ringsend and Irishtown from the Grand Canal, Dublin.

Signed: J H Campbell 1809
Watercolour on paper, 44.6 x 56.5 cms.
Transferred from the National Museum, 1966

The villages of Ringsend and Irishtown are situated on a spit of land east of the river Dodder. Their physical isolation is barely noticeable now but until the mid-seventeenth century the only access to this once prosperous fishing community at high tide was from the south. Even at low tide the direct route to Dublin across the slob lands was unpleasant. In about 1650 a bridge was erected but no sooner had it been completed than the river altered its course rendering it useless until the water was trained back to its original channel. This bridge was destroyed in a flood in 1782; it was replaced four years later but in 1802 the new bridge was also swept away. A sturdy single-arched bridge of mountain granite was erected shortly afterwards and has survived to date.

The presence of a bridge reduced the dangers involved in crossing the Dodder estuary. However it remained a quite self-contained district attracting, over the next two centuries a number of religious and secular public buildings to meet the needs of the growing population of the by now combined villages. By 1837 there were three churches, four schools, a dispensary and a shop which supplied the poor with items at reduced cost.

John Henry Campbell painted this view when the villages were still a unit some distance from the city. Since then both extensive land reclamation and development of the city have disguised their natural boundaries.

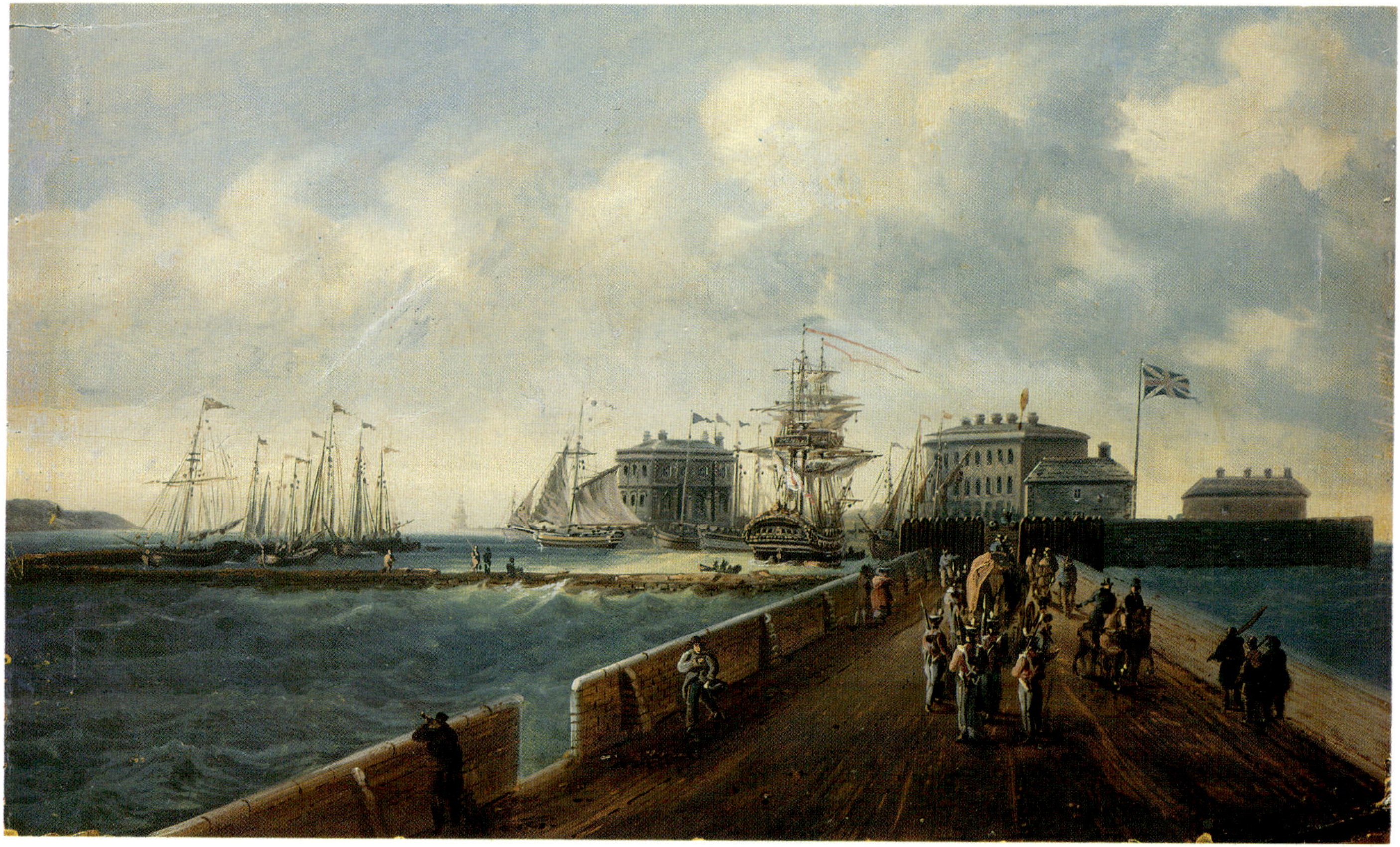

WILLIAM SADLER, (1782-1839)

The Pigeon House, Dublin.

Oil on panel, 29 x 41 cms.
Presented, Capt. G. O'Grady, 1911

The peculiar name of the Pigeon House, which became a hostelry in the mid-18th century, was probably derived from its first caretaker, John Pidgeon. Towards the end of the century, as local and international tensions increased, the area developed as a military base providing a landing position for troops as well as a retreat in the event of local hostilities. The basin, on the left of the wall in this view, was under construction in 1790; it was the principal dock for commercial as well as military ships for about twenty years until the development of Howth Harbour. Its brief commercial life is explained by the fact that at low tide there was insufficient water in the basin for docking; consequently domestic passengers who had already suffered a tedious sea journey from Britain, frequently had to wait up to three hours in Dublin Bay before coming ashore.

Despite the fall off in business after 1810 the hostelry continued to function amid the military activity until 1848 when its manageress, Mrs. Tunstal, retired. The Military remained in the Pigeon House until the end of the century. It was then sold to Dublin Corporation and is now part of the Electricity Supply Board's coal-fired power station. The land on either side of the wall has since been reclaimed and the Pigeon House is no longer such a prominent feature on the coastline.

William Sadler painted many small views of Dublin. This painting was probably executed during that brief period when the basin operated as a major commercial harbour.

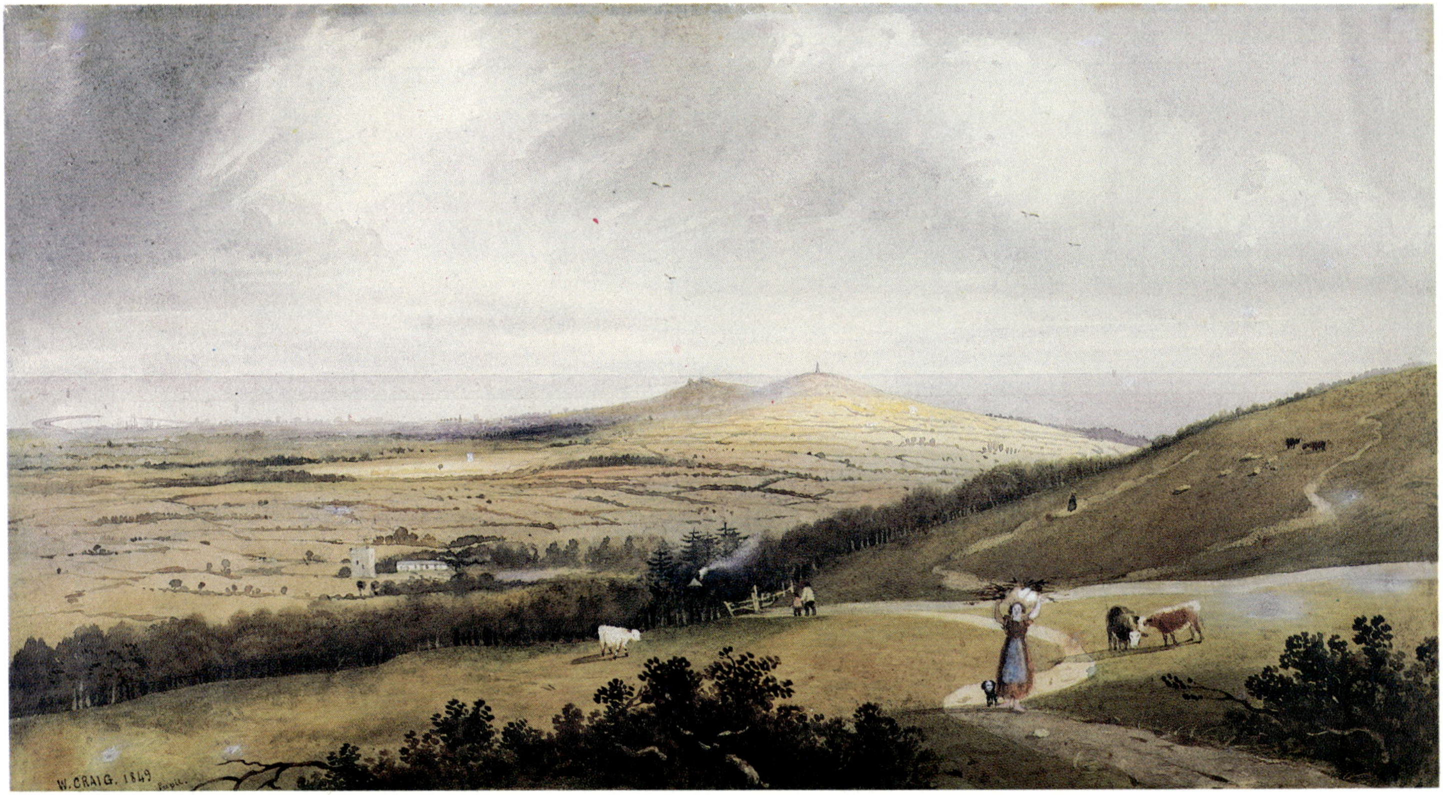

WILLIAM CRAIG, (1829-1875)

Kingstown (now Dún Laoghaire) Harbour and Killiney Hill Obelisk from Carrickmines, Co. Dublin.

Signed: W. Craig 1849.
Watercolour on paper, 26.6 x 48 cms.
Transferred from the National Museum, 1966

Dunleary or Dún Laoghaire was between 1821 and 1920 called Kingstown in commemoration of the embarkation of King George IV from the harbour after his state visit to Dublin. A granite obelisk was constructed near the eastern pier to mark the visit. The great harbour, built between 1817 and 1859, was designed by John Rennie (1761-1821) and cost £825,000. Its construction was a major feat of 19th century marine engineering. The granite rock was taken from nearby Dalkey Hill. The first railway in Ireland ran between Westland Row and Kingstown and opened on 17th December 1834.

Killiney Hill at four hundred and eighty feet affords a magnificent view of Howth, Dún Laoghaire, Dublin Bay and the two Sugar Loaf mountains and on its summit stands the obelisk which was erected in 1741 and bears the inscription: 'Last year being hard with the poor, the wall around these hills and this were erected by Mr. John Mapas, Esq. June 1742'. The obelisk now stands in Victoria Park, opened in 1887 and dedicated to public use by Prince Albert in memory of Queen Victoria's jubilee.

William Craig, a landscape artist, was born in Dublin in 1829. He entered the Royal Dublin Society Schools in 1847 and exhibited for the first time at the Royal Hibernian Academy in the same year. He went to America in 1863 where he was a founder member of the American Society of Watercolour Painters. He was drowned accidentally on August 26th 1875.

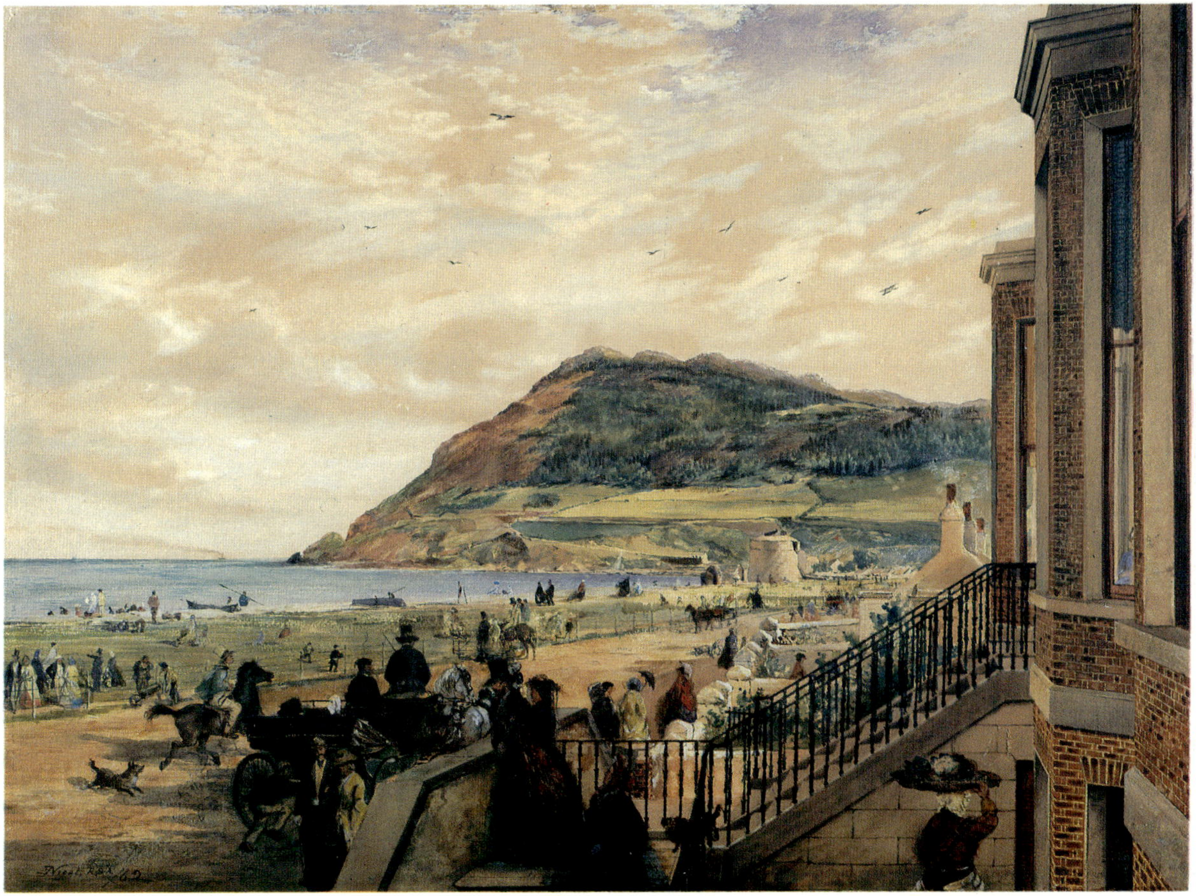

ERSKINE NICOL (1825-1904)

The Seafront at Bray, Co. Wicklow.

Signed and dated: EN (Mono, E. inverted)icol. R.S.A./62.
Pencil and watercolour with white highlights on paper, 48.2 x 64.3 cms.
Purchased, 1973

Bray is situated twelve miles south east of Dublin City and is known as the Gateway to Wicklow, the Garden of Ireland. The esplanade along the seafront, shown above, is one mile in length with a view at the end of Bray Head which consists of clay, slate and quartz and rises to a height of seven hundred and ninety one feet. The town itself is on the river Bray which serves as a natural boundary between the counties of Dublin and Wicklow.

Bray is famed as a holiday resort because of its close proximity to Dublin City and the accessibility of the Wicklow mountains and such tourist spots as Glendalough. The town itself owes much of its development to William Dargan (1799-1867), the railway entrepreneur who was involved in the 1853 International Exhibition in Dublin and whose statue by Thomas Farrell (1827-1900) stands on the lawn in front of the National Gallery of Ireland. The Martello Tower depicted here is no longer standing.

Erskine Nicol was born in Leith, Scotland, in July 1825 and was for some years apprenticed to a house decorator in Edinburgh. He spent a few years in Ireland between 1846 and 1850 teaching and painting portraits and after that he returned every year for a short spell until he retired to Scotland. He was known as a painter of humorous genre subjects and his most popular scenes were those of Irish peasant life. He died in 1904.

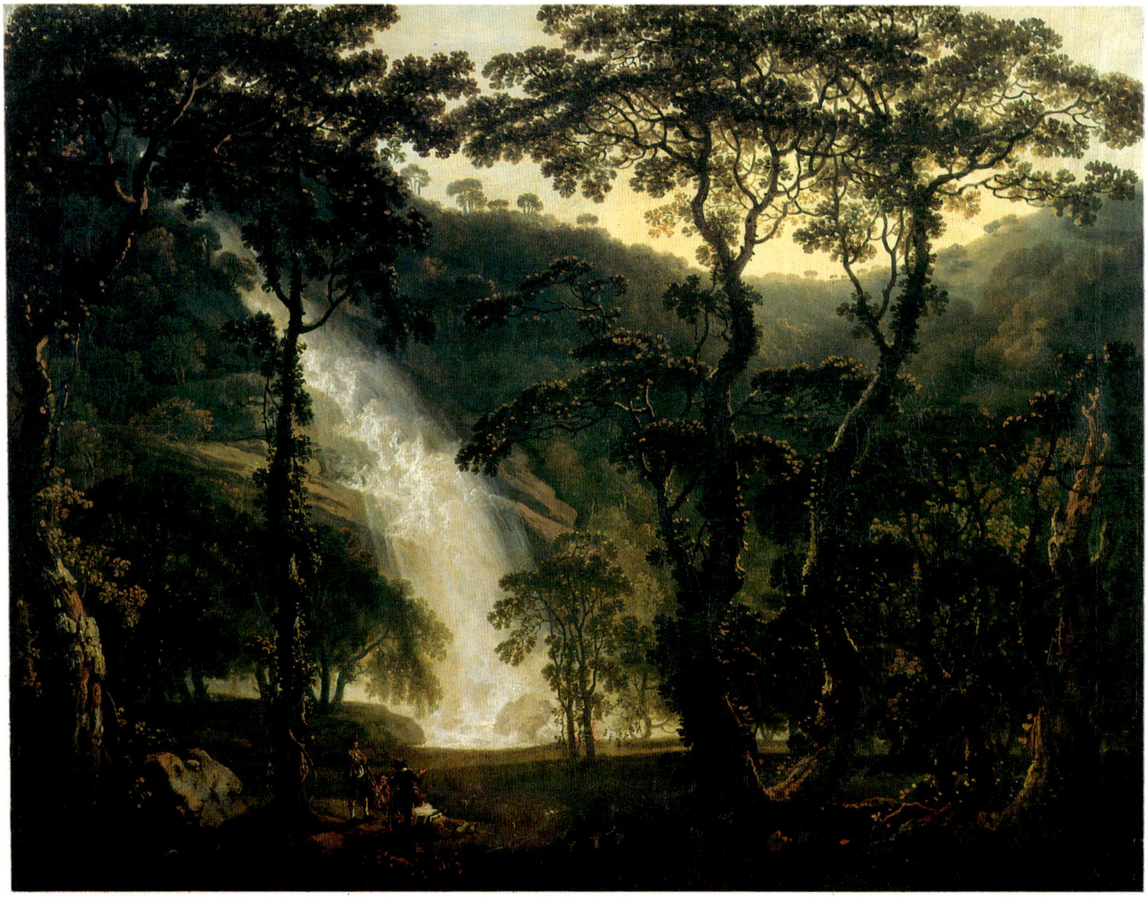

GEORGE BARRET, (c.1732-1784)

Powerscourt Waterfall.

Oil on canvas, 100 x 127 cms.
Purchased, 1880

Powerscourt Waterfall is situated in the Deerpark of Powerscourt Demesne near Enniskerry, Co. Wicklow. Powerscourt House, which was built by Richard Cassels 1731-40 and enlarged in the 19th century, was gutted by fire in 1974. It is said that when George IV came on a State visit to Ireland in 1821 a more spectacular view was arranged for his benefit by damming up the waterfall and building a special bridge. Fortunately the king missed the occasion, because when water was released the bridge was swept away by its force.

One of the highest in Britain or Ireland, the waterfall is caused by the Glenislorane river slipping almost perpendicularly three hundred and ninety eight feet down a precipice near the summits of the Djouce Mountain and War Hill. Further on the Glenislorane joins with the Glencree river which flows from Lough Bray, becoming firstly the Dargle river as it passes through the Dargle Valley, famous for Lovers' Leap, and finally the Bray river as it flows through Bray to the sea.

George Barret was born in the Liberties of Dublin c.1732. He emigrated to London and was instrumental in the foundation of the Royal Academy. Barret was a renowned artist in his day and, although he is said to have earned £2,000 per annum, he died in penury on May 29th 1784 and was buried in the graveyard of St. Mary's, Paddington.

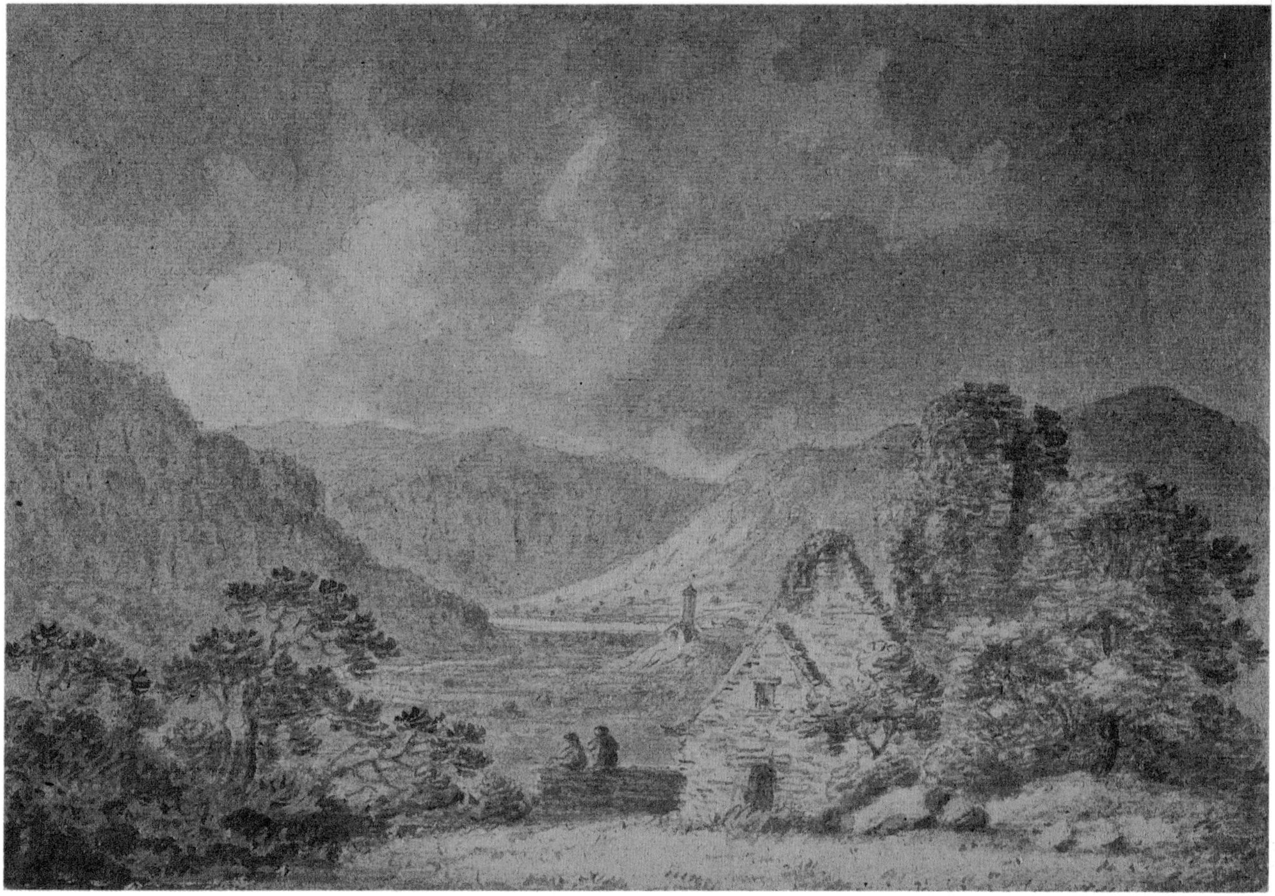

CHRISTOPHER MACHELL, (1747-1827)

St. Saviour's, St. Kevin's and the Lower Lake, Glendalough, Co. Wicklow.

Wash on buff paper, 31.5 x 40.4 cms.
Presented by Lady Valda Machell, 1951

Glendalough, the valley of the two lakes, in Co. Wicklow is one of the most important monastic sites in Ireland. St. Kevin, who died in 617, is credited with its foundation and St. Laurence O'Toole was Abbot of Glendalough between 1153 and 1162 before becoming Archbishop of Dublin. Restoration of the site, which is a National Monument, was begun in the 1870s by the Office of Public Works and the foundations of St. Kieran's Church, a short distance south east of St. Kevin's Church, were uncovered at this period.

Glendalough is also known as the City of the Seven Churches, two of which are depicted above. St. Kevin's Church or Kitchen has a small belfry, twenty six feet high, attached to it and a stone roof similar to that of St. Cormac's Chapel at the Rock of Cashel. Legend has it that it was the oratory and dormitory of St. Kevin himself. It served as the local Catholic church between 1810 and 1850, being the only church in the area with a roof. St. Saviour's Church is said to have been founded by St. Laurence O'Toole in 1162. It is almost half a mile from the main site on the south bank of the river Glendasan and in this view obscures the round tower.

Little is known of the artist, Christopher Machell. He was born in Westmoreland in 1747 and served on the British side as a major in the American War of Independence, losing an arm. Apart from being an artist, he was a skilful musician and a botanist. He died in 1827.

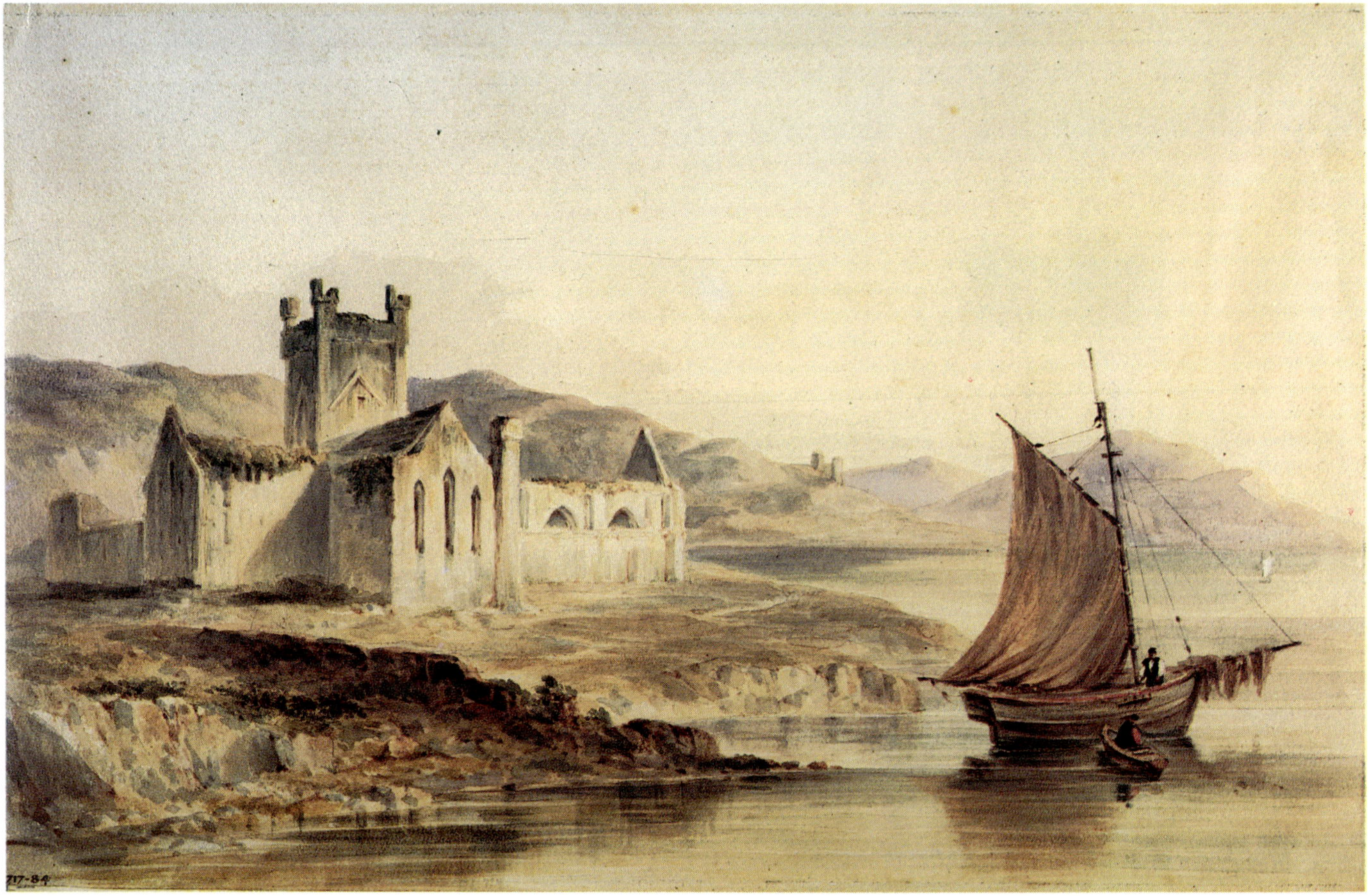

HENRY BROCAS SENIOR, (1766-1838)

Dunbrody Abbey, Co. Wexford.

Watercolour on paper, 32 x 49 cms.
Transferred from the National Museum, 1966

Dunbrody Abbey, beside the estuary of the river Suir in Co. Wexford, was founded for the Cistercians between 1175 and 1178 by Henry de Montemarisco, 1st Abbot, uncle of Richard, Earl of Pembroke (Strongbow) and Marshal of Henry II. The Abbey itself was built from about 1210 onwards by the English Cistercians of St. Mary's Abbey in Dublin and the central tower was added in the 15th century. The Cistercian order was founded in Burgundy in 1098 as a reaction to the excesses of many contemporary monasteries. The monks adopted a life of austerity and simplicity, dedicating themselves to poverty, labour, private prayer and contemplation. The first Cistercian Abbey in Ireland was at Mellifont, which dates from 1142.

Dunbrody Abbey is austere in the Cistercian tradition of utility and simplicity and is cruciform in shape, following the orthodox Cistercian layout. It is also one of the longest Cistercian Abbeys in Ireland at one hundred and ninety five feet in length and thirty four feet in width internally. The south arcade of the nave collapsed in 1852, but the forty foot high north wall remains. It is now a National Monument.

Henry Brocas Senior was a landscape painter who worked chiefly in watercolour and was self taught. He was also a prolific engraver and contributed to various magazines. He was Master of the Landscape and Ornament School of the Royal Dublin Society between 1801 and 1838, when he died on October 20th at the age of seventy four.

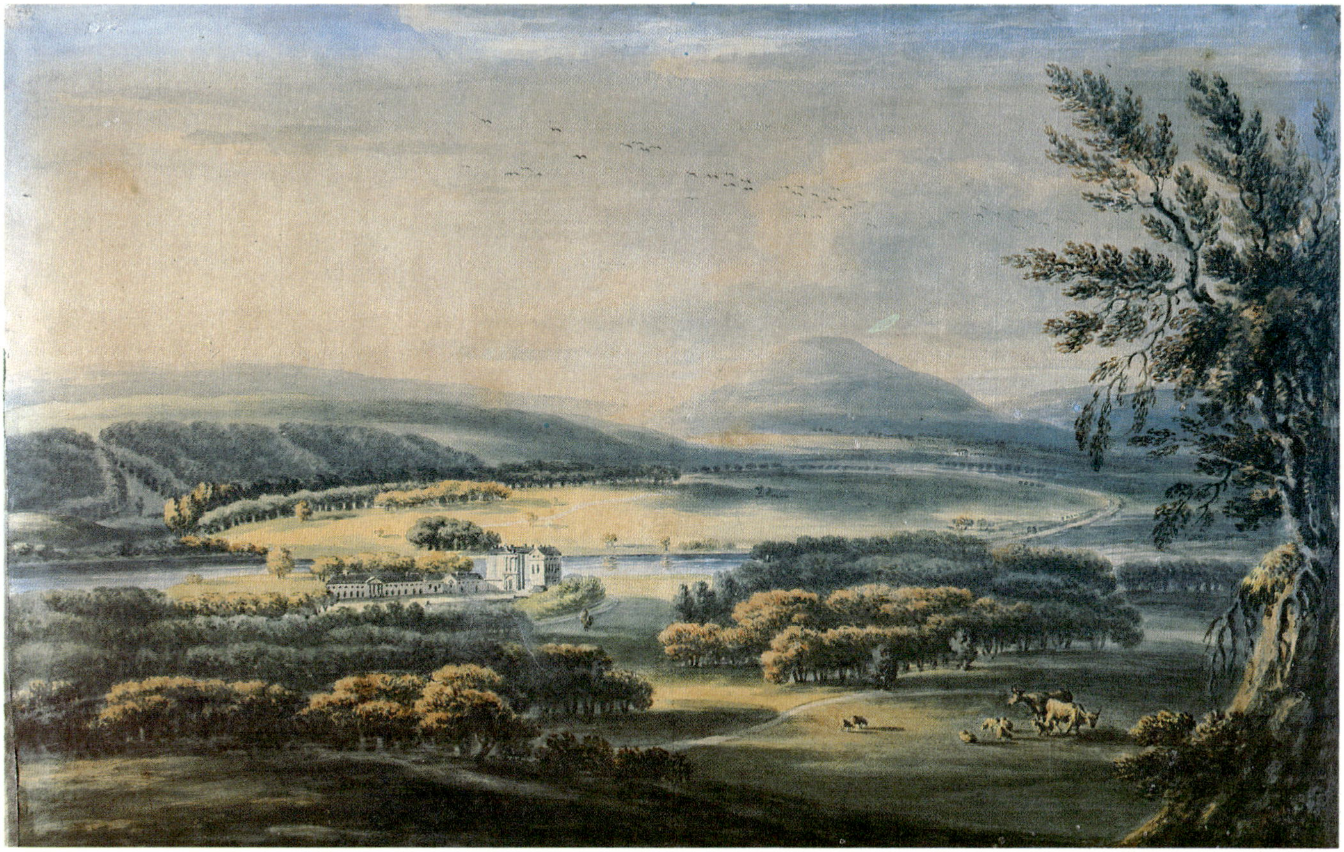

THOMAS SAUTELLE ROBERTS, (1760-1826).

Curraghmore House, Portlaw, Co. Waterford.

Watercolour on paper, 44 x 64 cms.
Purchased, 1979

Curraghmore House, Co. Waterford incorporates a Medieval tower from the old castle of the family of Le Poer or Power and a house which was in existence in 1654, which were remodelled and enlarged in the eighteenth century. The three storey house, seven bays wide with a small inner courtyard, has an enormous forecourt unmatched in the rest of Ireland, built by Thomas Sautelle Roberts' father, the Waterford architect, John Roberts (1716-1796).

The billiard room ceiling is thought to be the work of Philip and Paul Francini (fl. 1730-1760) and the grisaille paintings on the ceiling of the drawing-room and the walls of the dining-room are by Peter De Gree (1751-1789). Some of the decoration in these two rooms is also attributed to Antonio Zucchi (1726-1795), husband of Angelica Kauffman. This landscape was painted before Curraghmore House was refaced in the Classical style in the mid-nineteenth century.

Thomas Sautelle Roberts, younger brother of Thomas Roberts (1748-1778), was born in Waterford in 1760. Apprenticed to the architect Thomas Ivory (d. 1786) before turning to landscape painting in the 1770s, he exhibited at the Royal Academy and British Institution and also at the first exhibition of the Royal Hibernian Academy at their premises in Abbey Street in 1826. Following an injury to his shoulder which prevented him using a paintbrush, he suffered severe depression and in 1826 he committed suicide in his house in Portobello, Dublin.

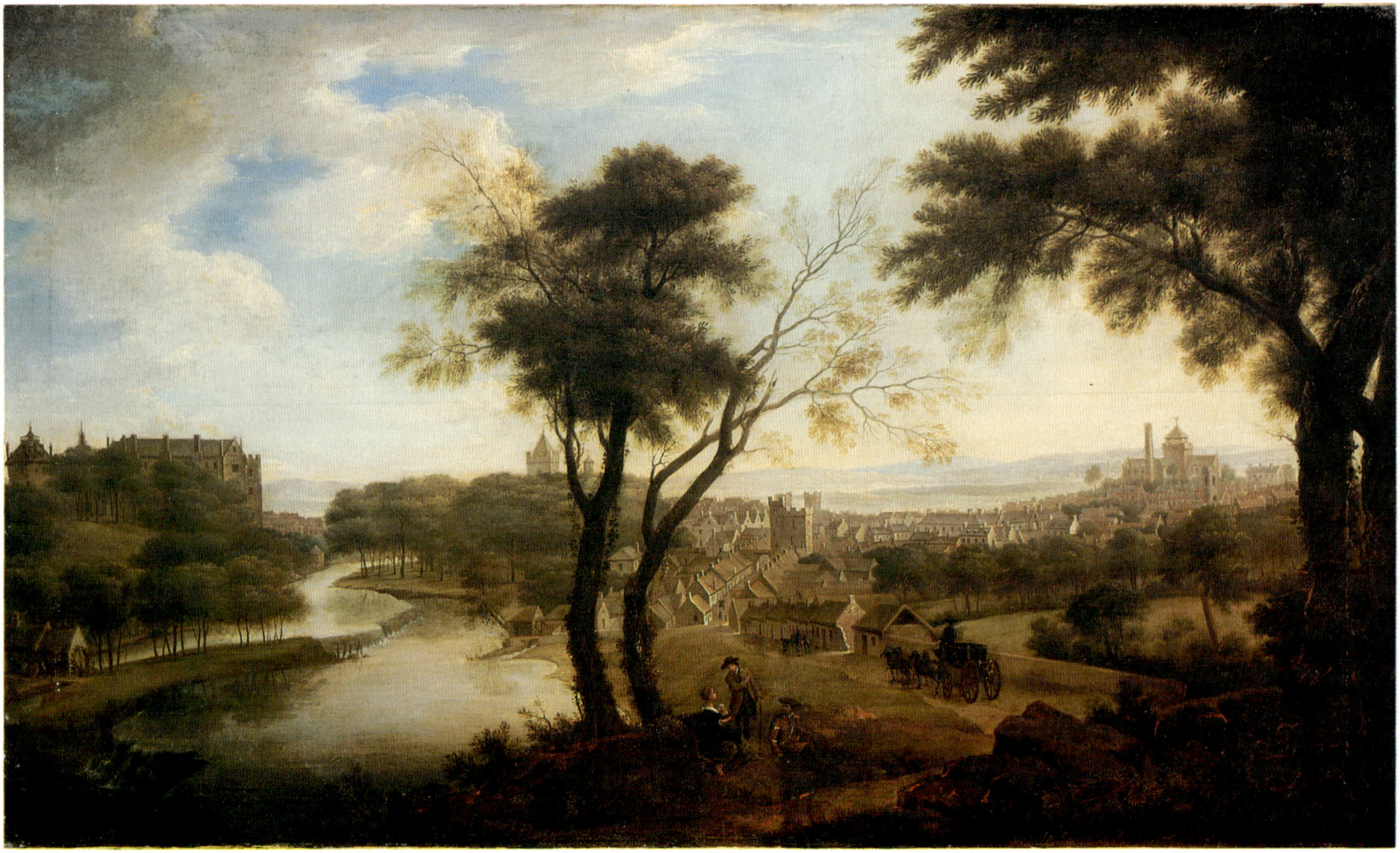

IRISH SCHOOL, (1760/1800)

A View of Kilkenny.

Oil on canvas, 95.2 x 150.5 cms.
Purchased, 1983

Many of the buildings featured in this view of Kilkenny from the east are still standing. On the extreme left is Kilkenny Castle, begun in the late 12th/early 13th century, rebuilt in the 17th century for the 1st Duke of Ormonde and heavily restored in the 19th century. It is now a National Monument. In the middle, above the trees, can be seen the medieval tower of St. Mary's which was replaced in 1819-20 and beside that the steeple of the Tholsel built in 1761 as the Exchange and Town Hall. On the right in Irishtown, the more ancient part of the city, is St. Canice's Cathedral which marks the site of the ancient monastery from which Kilkenny derives its name (Cill Choinnigh, Canice's Church). Besides it is the round tower which is the only surviving relic of the monastery. The conical cap was replaced by low battlements in the middle ages. The central tower of the cathedral, which can be seen clearly, has been removed.

Kilkenny was conferred with the rank and dignity of a city by James I in 1609. It is divided by the river Nore into two unequal parts. Kilkenny was one of the principal meeting places of the Anglo-Irish parliament and it was here that the notorious 'Statutes of Kilkenny' were enacted in 1367, which tried to prevent the gaelicisation of the Anglo-Norman community.

The identity of the artist who painted this picture is unknown, but from the combined evidence of the buildings and the style, it can be attributed to the Irish School and dated between 1760 and 1800.

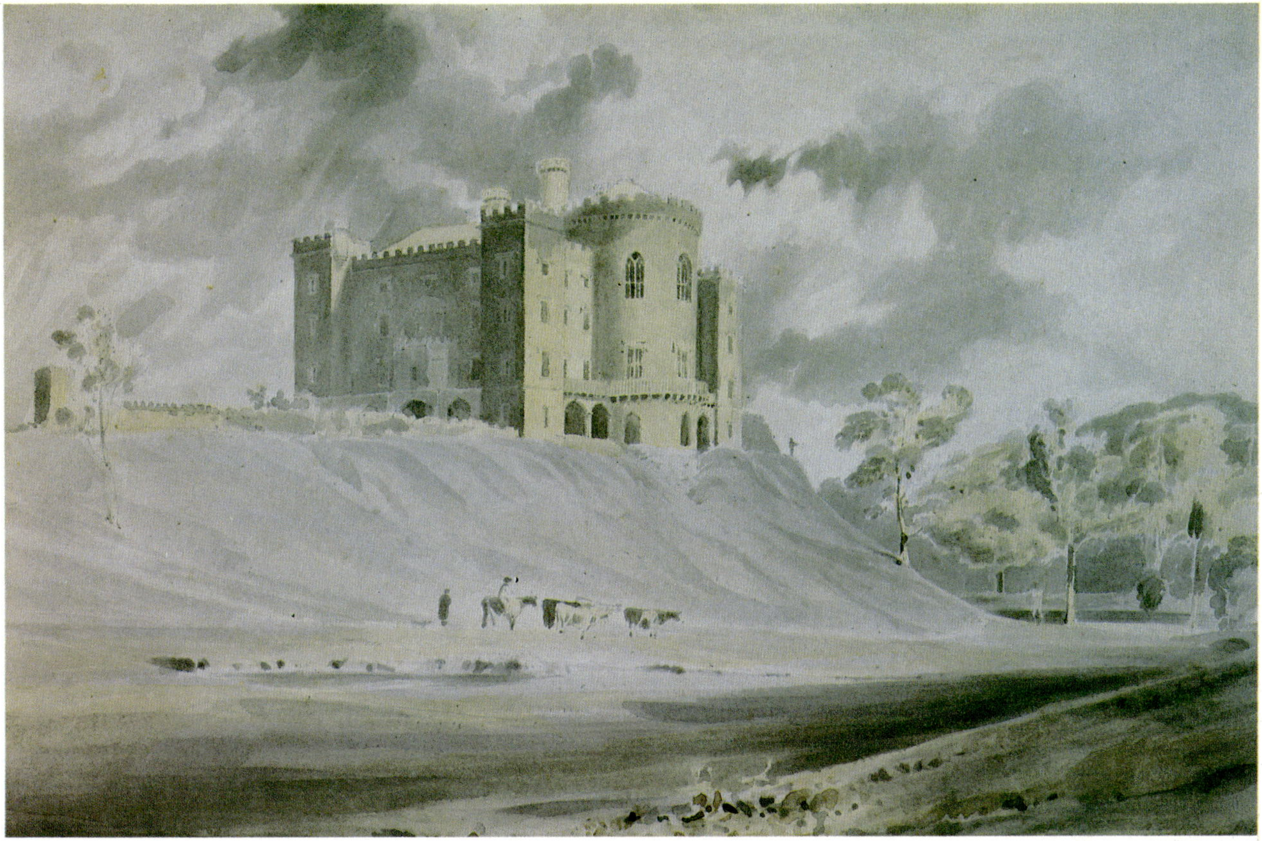

GEORGE PETRIE, (1789-1866)

Slane Castle, Co. Meath.

Signed: Geo Petrie Del^{t}.
Wash on paper, 18 x 26.7 cms.
Bequeathed by Miss M. Stokes, 1900

Slane Castle, the seat of the Marquess Conyngham, occupies an elevated site on the banks of the Boyne river. It was built on the foundations of a medieval castle, fortress of the Flemings, Lords of Slane, a Catholic family of Norman origin who were prominent in the area until they lost their lands following the insurrection of 1641. The Castle was subsequently acquired by the Conyngham family and rebuilt by William, the second Earl Conyngham, who succeeded his uncle to the title in 1781.

In 1785 James Wyatt, an English architect acclaimed for his skill in restoration architecture popular at the time, was called upon to reconstruct the old castle; the existing building was largely demolished and the present castle was built on the foundation. Essentially classical in design it is symmetrical in its elevations; the gothic features, clearly apparent in this view, include battlements, a small square tower at each corner, and a bow in the centre of the front overlooking the river which is raised above the rest of the building to form a round tower. Restoration of the castle was completed by Francis Johnston who designed the entrance and carried out significant alterations to the interior. Other highly regarded architects consulted about the building at various times included 'Capability' Brown and James Gandon.

The dead-straight road from Dublin to Slane is said to have been made specially for George IV who stayed in the Castle on two occasions, once as Prince of Wales and later as King. George Petrie's splendid view of Slane Castle was one of ninety-six illustrations which he supplied for Cromwell's *Excursions through Ireland* in 1820.

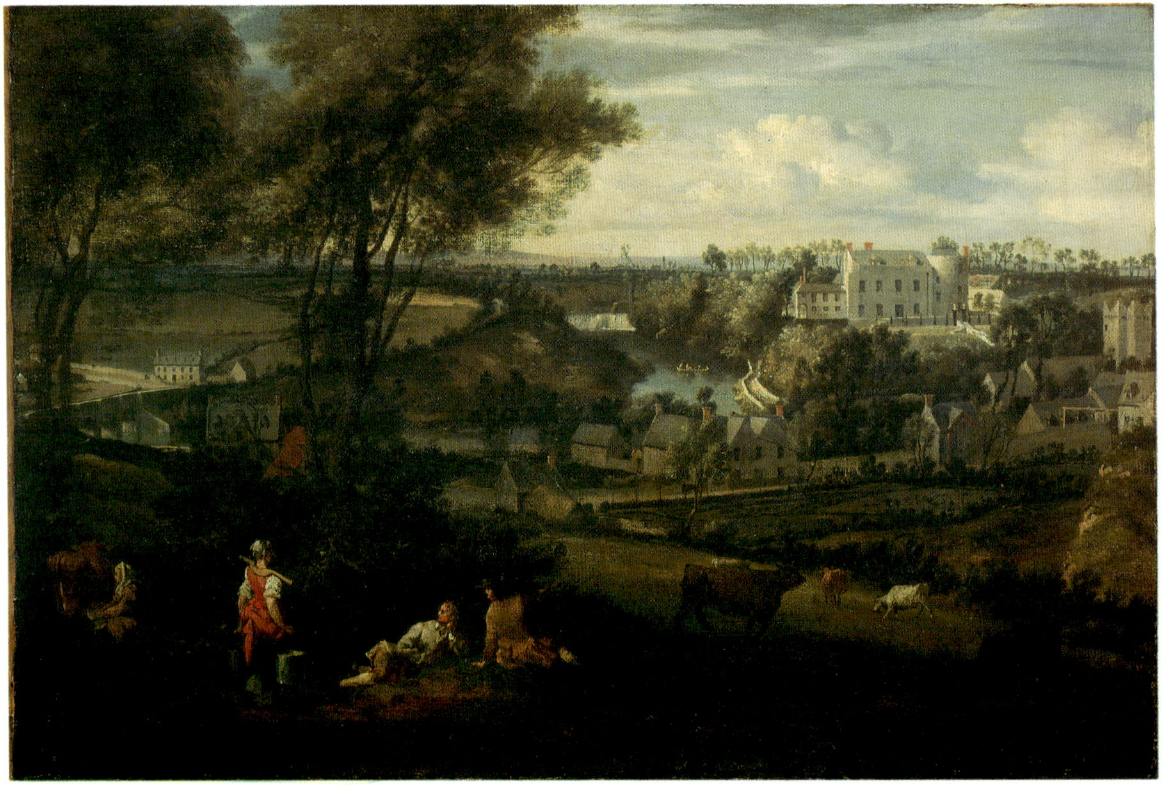

IRISH SCHOOL, (c.1750)

Leixlip Castle, Co. Kildare.

Oil on canvas, 50 x 72 cms.
Purchased, 1910

Leixlip Castle was founded in the late 12th century on lands granted to Adam de Hereford, a follower of Strongbow. Built high upon a rock above the junction of the Rye Water and the river Liffey, it was one of the castles which marked the border of the 'Pale', — the rich lands surrounding Dublin in which the authority of the English Government prevailed. During the turbulent times of the 15th and 16th centuries the crown maintained control over the possession of this key fortress; in 1569 it was granted to Sir Nicholas Whyte, Master of the Rolls, and remained in the family's possession until 1731 when it was sold to William Conolly, nephew of Speaker Conolly of Castletown House.

Documentary evidence for the development of Leixlip Castle is scarce. The dominant feature of the castle, the massive round tower on the right of the building in this view, dates from the 12th century; the wing forming a projection on the entrance front was part of an 18th century development which also included extensive renovation of the interior. Few alterations have been made since then, perhaps because it was seldom occupied by the owner. The Conollys let it to a series of tenants including Lord Townshend, Viceroy of Ireland (1767-1772) who used it as a summer residence. George Cavendish, a later tenant, is thought to have added the unobtrusive battlements in 1837. Lady Decie, whose husband purchased the castle in 1914 intended to make extensive alterations but troubles abroad and in Ireland interfered with her plans. The castle has changed ownership twice since that time.

The name 'Leixlip' is derived from the old Norse name of the Salmon-Leap, 'Laxhlaup', in the vicinity of the Castle; the Salmon-Leap was a favourite inland resort of Dubliners in the 18th and 19th centuries; it is now harnessed by a power station. This early Irish landscape depicts Leixlip Castle on the small hill overlooking the confluence of the rivers and the village of Leixlip. The artist is unknown but the picture was engraved in 1750.

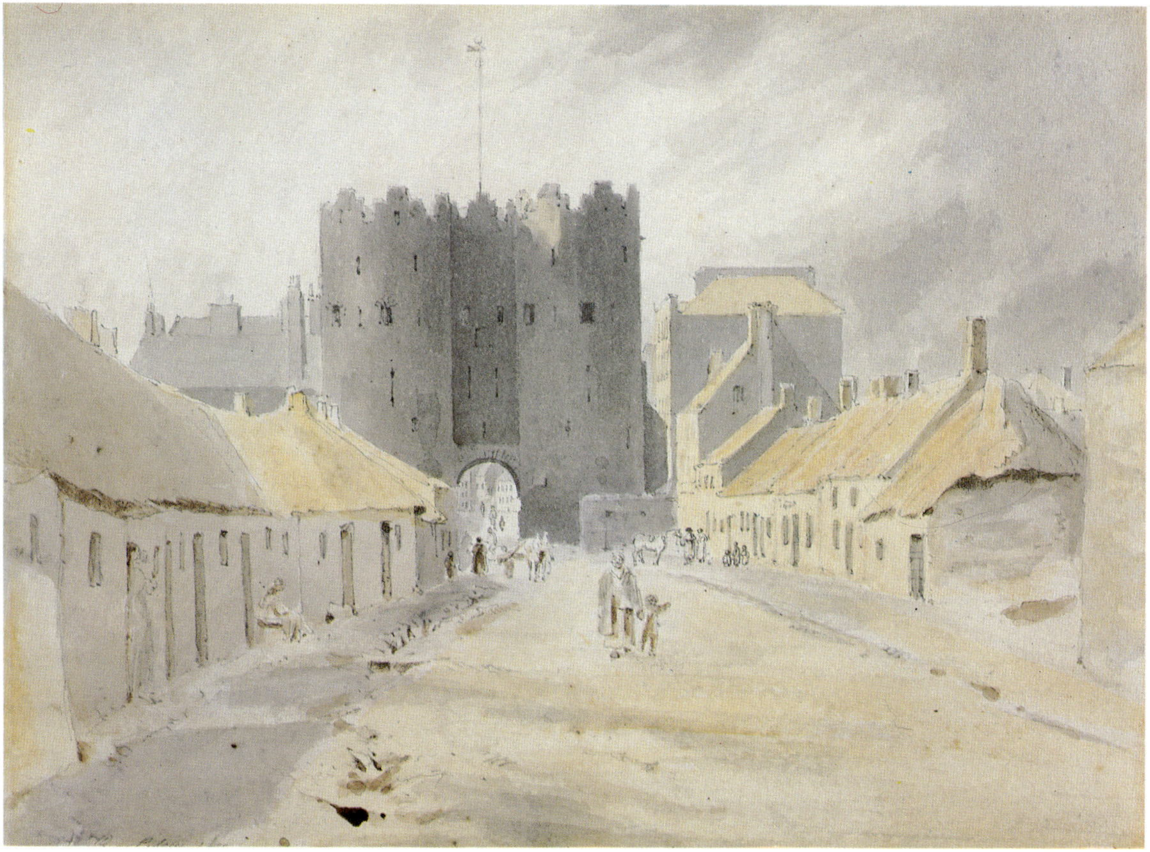

GEORGE PETRIE, (1789-1866)

St. Lawrence's Gate, Drogheda, Co. Louth.

Signed and dated: Geo Petrie 1819.
Pencil and watercolour on paper, 17.8 x 23.4 cms.
Bequeathed by Miss M. Stokes, 1900

Drogheda, on the river Boyne, was walled and fortified by the Anglo-Normans in the 13th century and rapidly became one of the major ports of Ireland. Throughout the Middle Ages the town was under constant threat of attack. The town burgesses, who had been granted privileges similar to those granted to the burgesses of Dublin, were given additional concessions to maintain and increase the fortifications. Little now remains of the defences.

The view of St. Lawrence's gate by Petrie is in fact a drawing of its barbican. The gate, which stood behind the barbican, has long since vanished although the barbican itself remains largely intact. This formidable defence dates from the mid-13th century and was known simply as the East Gate until the mid-14th century. It consists of two almost circular drum towers with four floors in each and a crenellated parapet at the top. A flight of steps leads to each tower and a bridge at parapet level enables movement between the two. With a defensible front on both sides it could have held off an attack from inside the town as well as from the outside. The entrance had a portcullis and wooden gates.

In the 17th century Drogheda fell under siege a number of times, the most famous of which was the attack by the Parliamentary troops under Cromwell in 1649. Since then the fortifications have fallen into decay; all that remains is a portion of the wall on the west side, the barbican of St. Lawrence's Gate and a portion of the wall near it. The barbican, which stands in St. Lawrence's Street, is amongst the finest examples of medieval town defences to survive in Ireland.

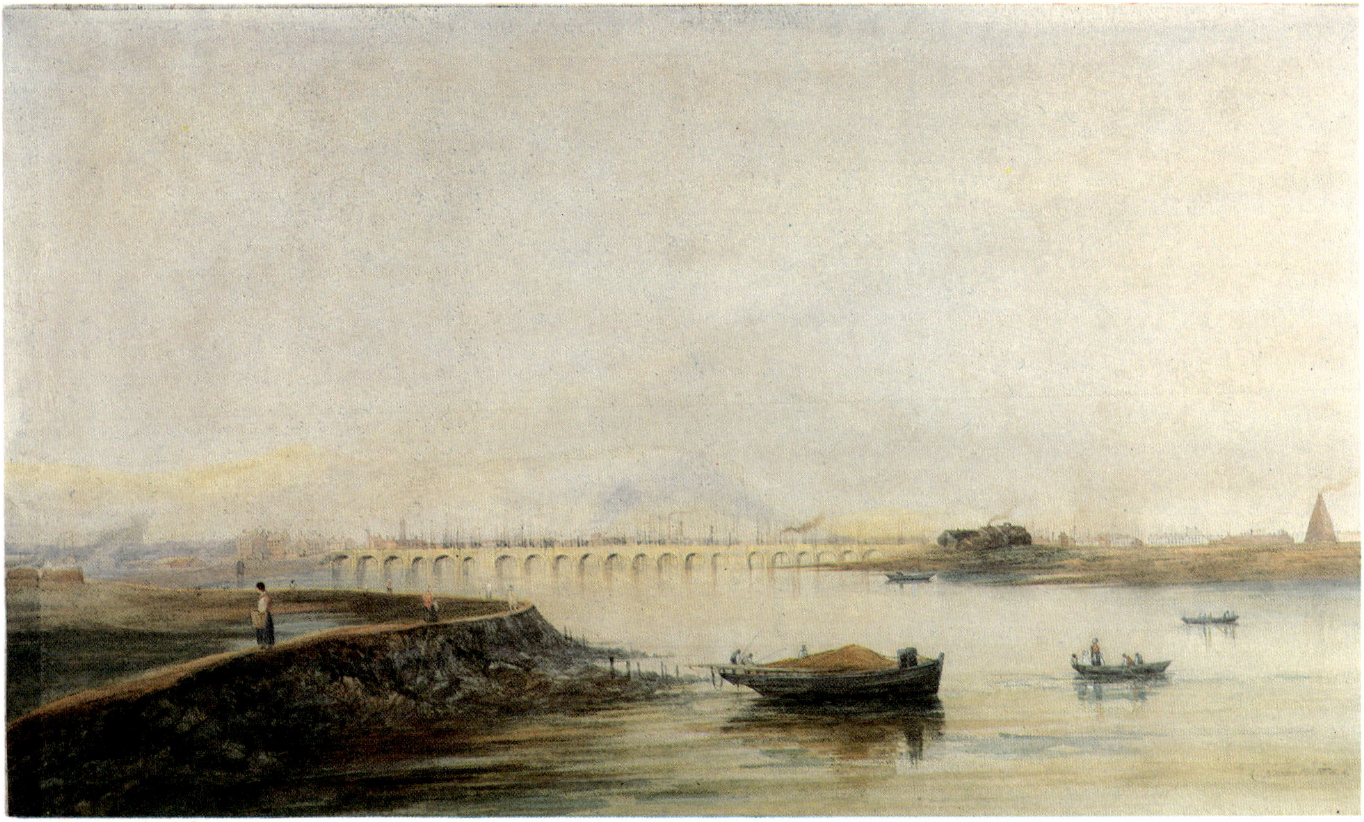

ANDREW NICHOLL, (1804-1886)

The Long Bridge, Belfast and Cave Hill, Co. Antrim.

Signed: A. Nicholl R.H.A.
Pencil and watercolour on paper, 51.5 x 82.5 cms.
Presented by the Rev. J.R. McKee, 1922

The Long Bridge, spanning the tidal mud flats of the river Lagan, was built in 1686 and connected Belfast in Co. Antrim to the suburb of Ballymacarret in Co. Down. The bridge, long, narrow and with twenty one arches, was built near the mouth of the river Lagan where it flows into Belfast Lough. It was damaged in 1689 by the crossing of the artillery of Marshal Schomberg, King William of Orange's commander, shortly before the Battle of the Boyne. It was replaced in 1842-43 by Queen's Bridge under the superintendence of the county surveyors, John Frazer and Charles Lanyon. The 'new' bridge is still there, having been widened in 1886.

Cave Hill, the most eastern of the mountain chain to the north of Belfast, is depicted in the distance. On the summit stands the stronghold of Brian Mac Airt O'Neill, slain in 1601 by Lord Deputy Mountjoy, and from here can be seen the Isle of Man, the shores and mountains of Scotland and a large portion of the counties of Antrim, Down, Armagh, Derry and Donegal. It was here that Wolfe Tone and his comrades made the famous vow 'never to desist in our efforts until we have subverted the authority of England over our country' in 1794. Belfast's Zoological Gardens are now on the slopes of Cave Hill.

Andrew Nicholl, born in Belfast in 1804, manifested his artistic talent at an early age, but it was not until he had spent seven years' apprenticeship as a compositor for the *Northern Whig* that he was able to support himself by his paintings and teaching. He died in London in 1886.

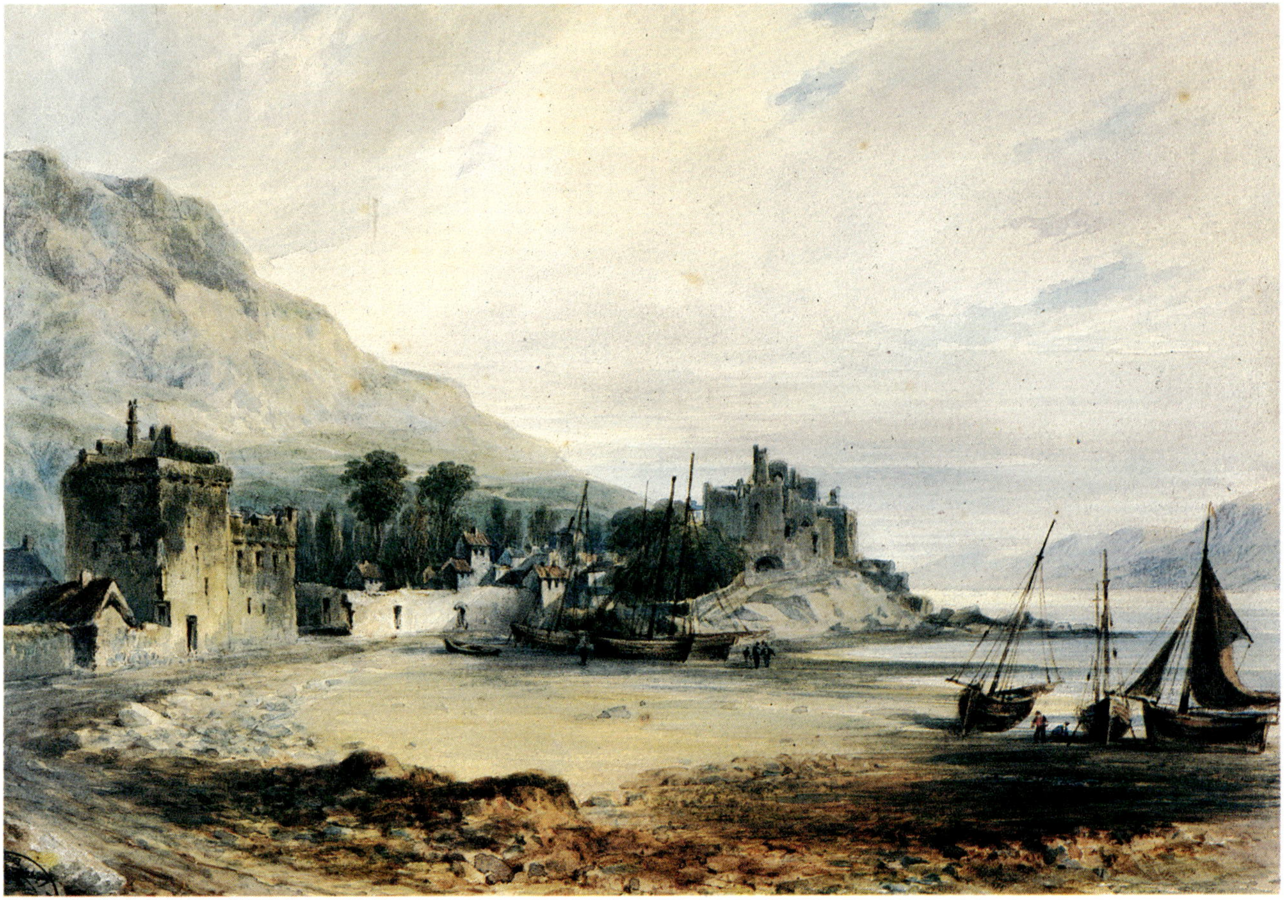

HENRY BROCAS SENIOR,
(1766-1838)

Carlingford Castle, Co. Louth.

Watercolour on paper, 29.5 x 42 cms.
Transferred from the National Museum, 1966

Carlingford Castle, known also as King John's Castle because he stayed there for three days in 1210, was built in the 12th century by Hugh de Lacy. The castle was built on the verge of a small cliff commanding the entrance to the harbour and the narrow pass between it and Slieve Foye which rises one thousand nine hundred and thirty five feet above the south shore of Carlingford Lough. It was an important border fortress of the English pale 'constantly exposed to the danger from the marauding attacks of the Irish enemy', but, because of its setting, no ramparts, moats or drawbridges were required.

The castle had to be adapted to the configuration of the rock site and is consequently D-shaped, with the curved part facing the slopes to the west and enclosing an open courtyard. A gateway set in this wall admitted only a single horseman at a time as a defence measure. A high wall running from north to south divides the site in two; the eastern wall dating from c.1261 and the western built somewhat earlier. The castle is now a National Monument. On the left is Taaffe's Castle, a 16th century fortified town house and an important example of a late towerhouse.

Henry Brocas Senior was born in 1766 and died in 1838. A landscape painter and engraver, he was father to Samuel Frederick (1792-1847), James Henry (1790-1846), William (1794-1868) and Henry (1798-1873) Brocas, all artists in their own right.

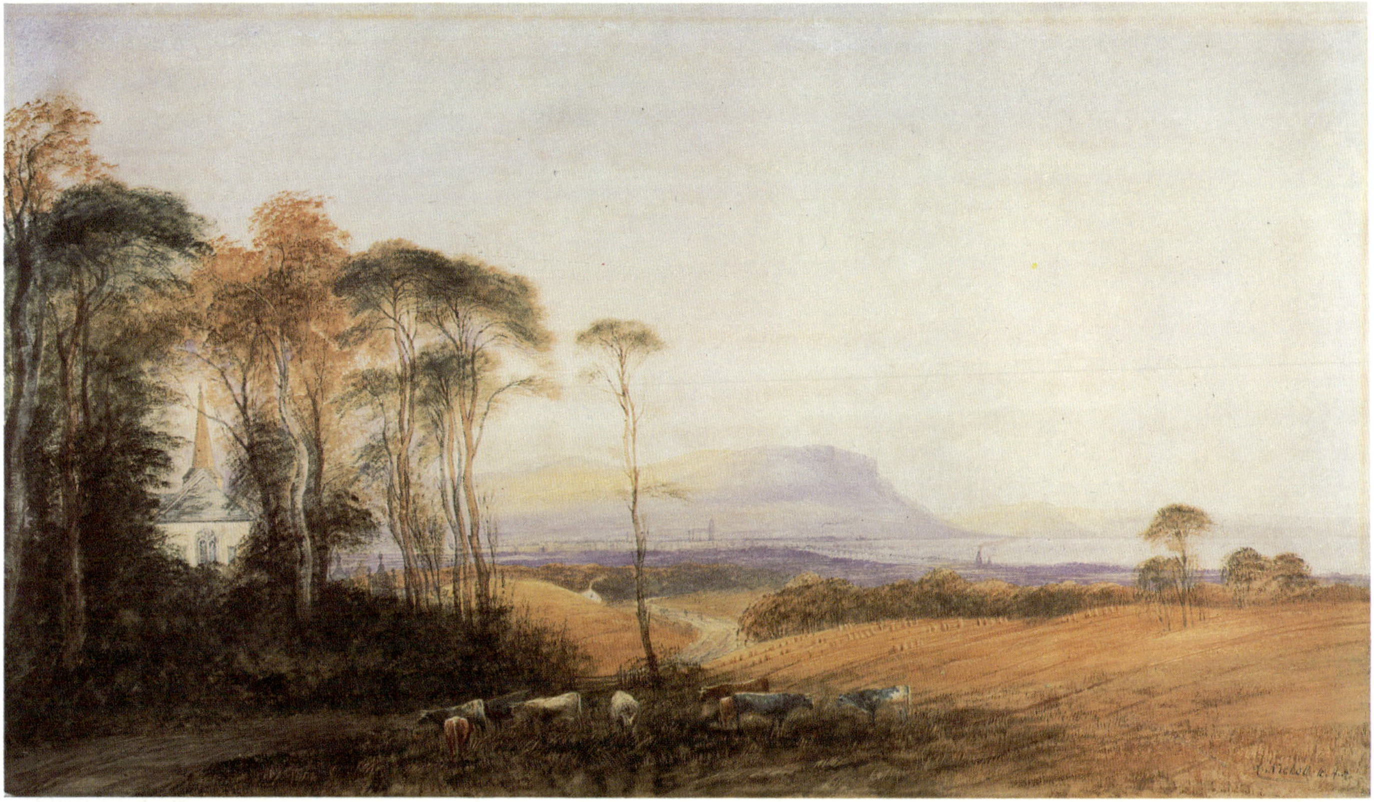

ANDREW NICHOLL, (1804-1886)

Belfast and Cave Hill, Co. Antrim, from Newtownbreda Church.

Signed: A. Nicholl R.H.A.
Watercolour on paper, 52 x 87.3 cms.
Transferred from the National Museum, 1966.

Newtownbreda Church, Co. Down, from where Nicholl painted this distant view of Belfast, can be seen on the left of this picture, partially hidden by trees. This early Georgian church was the work of Richard Cassels, born Flesse Kassel, Ireland's leading architect of the day who was also responsible for the Rotunda Hospital in Dublin. The church is described in Lewis' *Topographical Dictionary of Ireland* as '. . . a small but elegant edifice in the grecian style . . .' Charles Lanyon (1813-1889), who prepared designs for the National Gallery of Ireland in 1856 (which were not used), is buried in the churchyard.

The city of Belfast is approximately mid-way between Newtownbreda Church and Cave Hill, the other important feature in this view. Cave Hill, so-called because caves are hollowed out of the basalt rock of the mountain face, is close to Belfast Lough and is part of the mountain range north of the city. In Mr. and Mrs. Hall's *Ireland: Its Scenery, Character etc.* is the following: 'A singular peculiarity connected with Cave Hill was pointed out to us; seen from nearly every part of the southern suburbs, its outline resembles, in a very remarkable manner, the profile of Napoleon.'

Andrew Nicholl, born on April 4th 1804, was the son of Henry Nicholl, a bootmaker in Church Lane, Belfast and brother of William Nicholl (1794-1840), a painter in his own right. He was a founder member of the Belfast Association of Artists and he exhibited often in the Royal Hibernian Academy, becoming an associate in 1837 and a member in 1860. His time was divided between Belfast, Dublin and London with a period spent teaching in the Columbo Academy in Ceylon. He died at Camberwell Grove, London, on April 16th, 1886 and a retrospective exhibition of his work was held in Belfast in the same year.

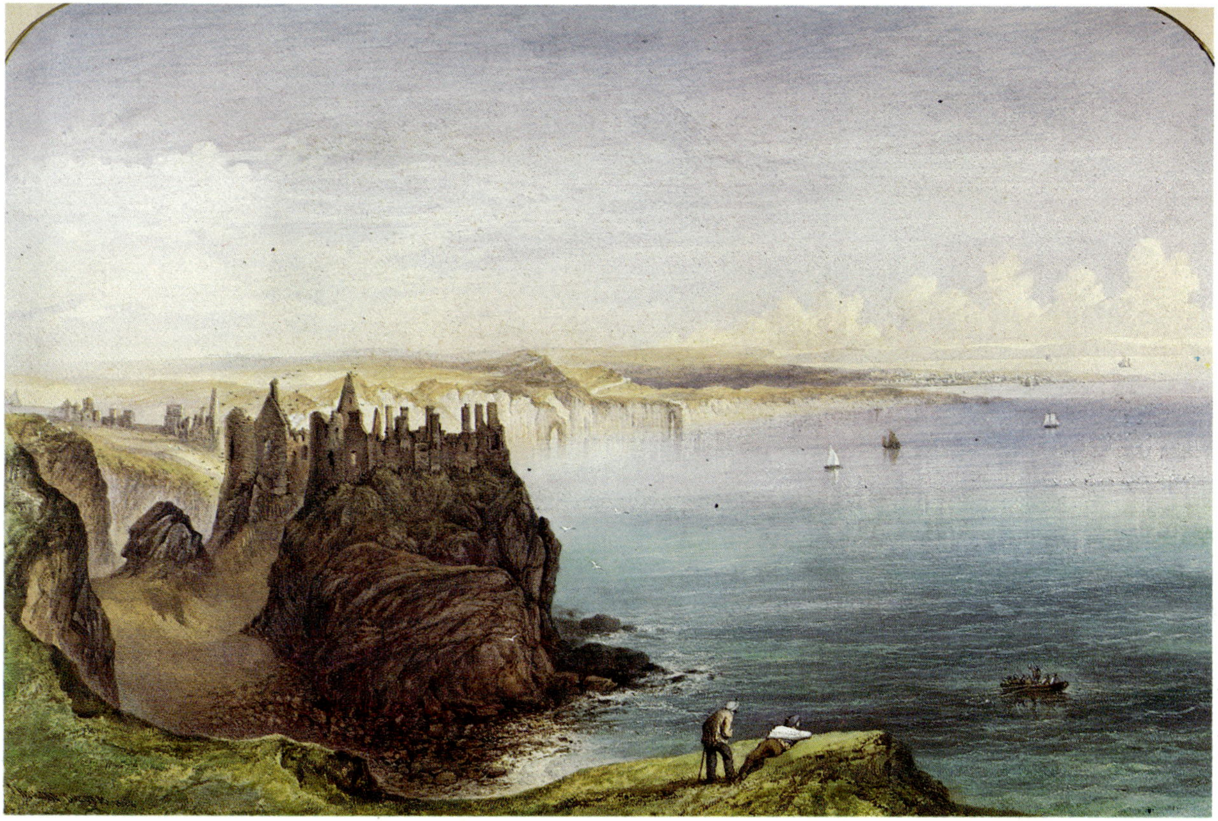

JAMES HOWARD BURGESS,
(1817-1890)

Dunluce Castle, Co. Antrim.

Signed and dated: J. Howard Burgess, 1866.
Watercolour on paper, 53 x 78.8 cms.
Presented by Rev. J.R. McKee, 1922

Dunluce Castle was described by one 19th century writer as '. . . without any exceptions, the grandest, romanticest, awfulest sea King's castle in broad Europe . . .', an opinion obviously shared by Burgess. His romantic view of the castle exaggerates its isolated position on a rocky promontory which is in the vicinity of the Giant's Causeway on the North Antrim coast. The castle would seem to have been a four sided fortress with a strong cylindrical tower at each corner, and was probably built in about 1300 by an Anglo-Norman lord on the site of an earlier fort. Two of the towers and part of the south curtain survive from this period. However, much of the ruin in this view is made up of the remains of extensive domestic quarters built in the 16th and 17th centuries.

The importance of the castle's strategic position on the northern coast is indicated by its recorded history. In the mid-16th century Sorley Boy McDonnell ousted the residing MacQuillan clan and despite being forcibly evicted on two occasions, once by the O'Neills, and later by the Lord Deputy, he was still in possession at the time of his death in 1589. His sons, Randal and James, succeeded him and in 1620 the former was created Earl of Antrim. Following the arrest of the Royalist 2nd Earl in 1642 the family moved out and the castle fell into decay. In 1928 the 7th Earl transferred the property to the Northern Ireland Government and it is now a National Monument.

Burgess, a draughtsman and miniature painter, practised in Belfast, Carrickfergus and Dublin for many years. He painted numerous landscapes in watercolour and twenty five of his illustrations were amongst those used in Halls *'Ireland: Its Scenery, Character, etc.*, published in 1841.

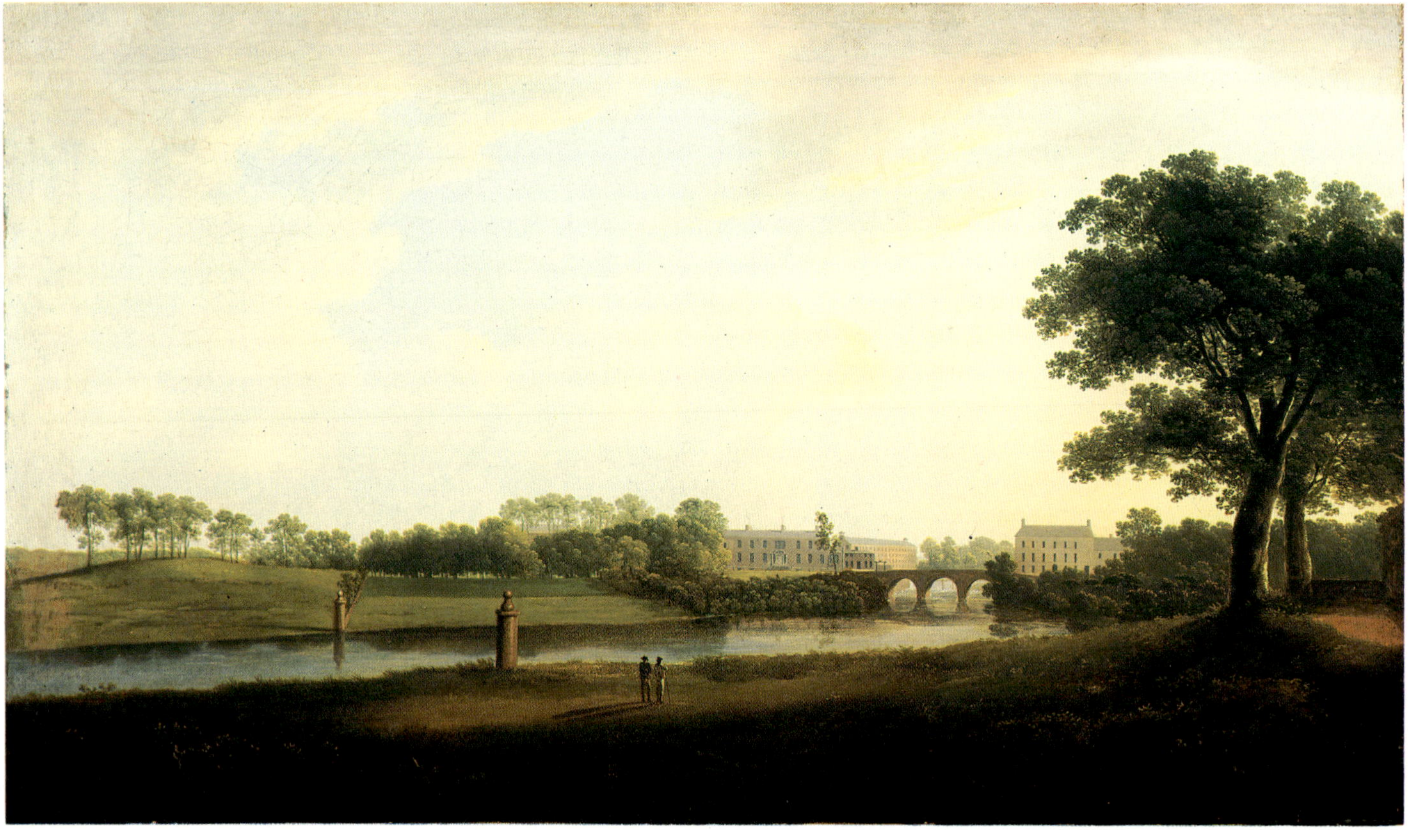

JAMES ARTHUR O'CONNOR, (1792-1841)

Ballinrobe House, Co. Mayo.

Oil on canvas, 42 x 71 cms.
Purchased, 1970

Ballinrobe House, or Robe Villa as it is referred to in Lewis' *Topographical Dictionary of Ireland*, is situated on the Robe river near Lough Mask in Co. Mayo. It was built by the Courtney Kenny family c.1740 close to their corn mill; the former family seat, Roxburgh, being too far away. It is a two storey Georgian house and is shown to the left of the three-arched bridge near the mill. It must have been altered in the late 18th or early 19th century, because above the Georgian fanlighted doorway is a Wyatt window, named after the British architect James Wyatt (1747-1813).

The Pleasure Grounds stretched from the house to the river when O'Connor painted this view, but now a road runs immediately in front of the house. When it was built, a tunnel was dug under the road to enable the family to use the pleasure grounds safely and easily.

James Arthur O'Connor, who was born in Dublin in 1792, painted this view (c.1818-1819) while he was being patronised by Lord Sligo and Lord Clanricarde, for both of whom he painted a number of views around Westport in Co. Mayo and Portumna in Co. Galway. This is an example of his early style and is one of a set of four paintings for the Courtney Kenny family at Ballinrobe now in the National Gallery of Ireland. O'Connor died in poverty in London on January 7th, 1841 and a subscription, headed by Albert, the Prince Consort, was started for his wife's benefit in 1845.

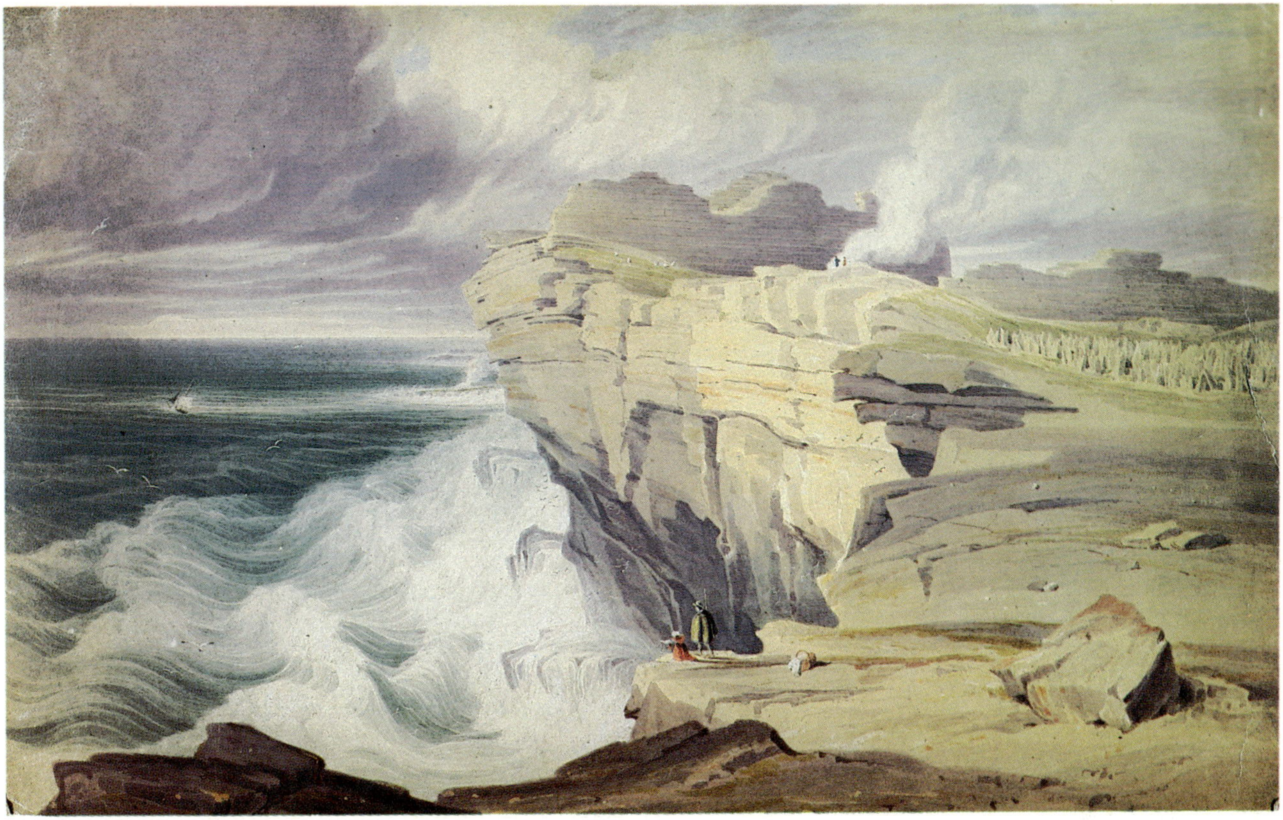

GEORGE PETRIE, (1789-1866)

Dun Aengus Fort, Inishmore, Aran Islands.

Watercolour on paper, 29.8 x 46.4 cms.
Provenance unknown.

Dun Aengus on the largest of the Aran Islands was described by Petrie as '. . . probably one of the most barbaric monuments in the west of Europe.' This atmospheric view of the fort emphasises its dramatic position on the summit of an overhanging cliff about three hundred feet above the Atlantic Ocean.

The defences of the ancient fort consist of four dry-stone wall ramparts forming roughly concentric semi-circles: a thick high terraced wall encloses the inner keep; outside this are two smaller walls; starting immediately under the third wall is a *chevaux-de-frise,* — thousands of limestone stakes placed upright in the ground designed to make access difficult for an approaching enemy. A considerable distance beyond this is a fourth, slightly weaker, rampart.

The date of construction and the history of the fort are unknown as is the origin of the name. The unusual location of the high fort has given rise to numerous theories as to its original function, one of the more romantic of which suggests that Aengus was a prince of the old conquered race, the Fir Bolgs, which was driven westwards by the invading force of Tuatha de Danann. In fact the name Dun Aengus was adopted in the 19th century by the Ordnance Survey on uncertain authority. Another theory, and one which Petrie subscribed to briefly, maintained that the fort was originally circular or oval and part of it had fallen away with the cliff; he abandoned this explanation as there was no evidence of recent subsidence.

In 1881 the Office of Public Works undertook the preservation of Dun Aengus and much of the structure now, including terraces and buttresses, dates from that time. Petrie journeyed to Inishmore on a number of occasions; he painted this view during one of his later visits in the 1850s.

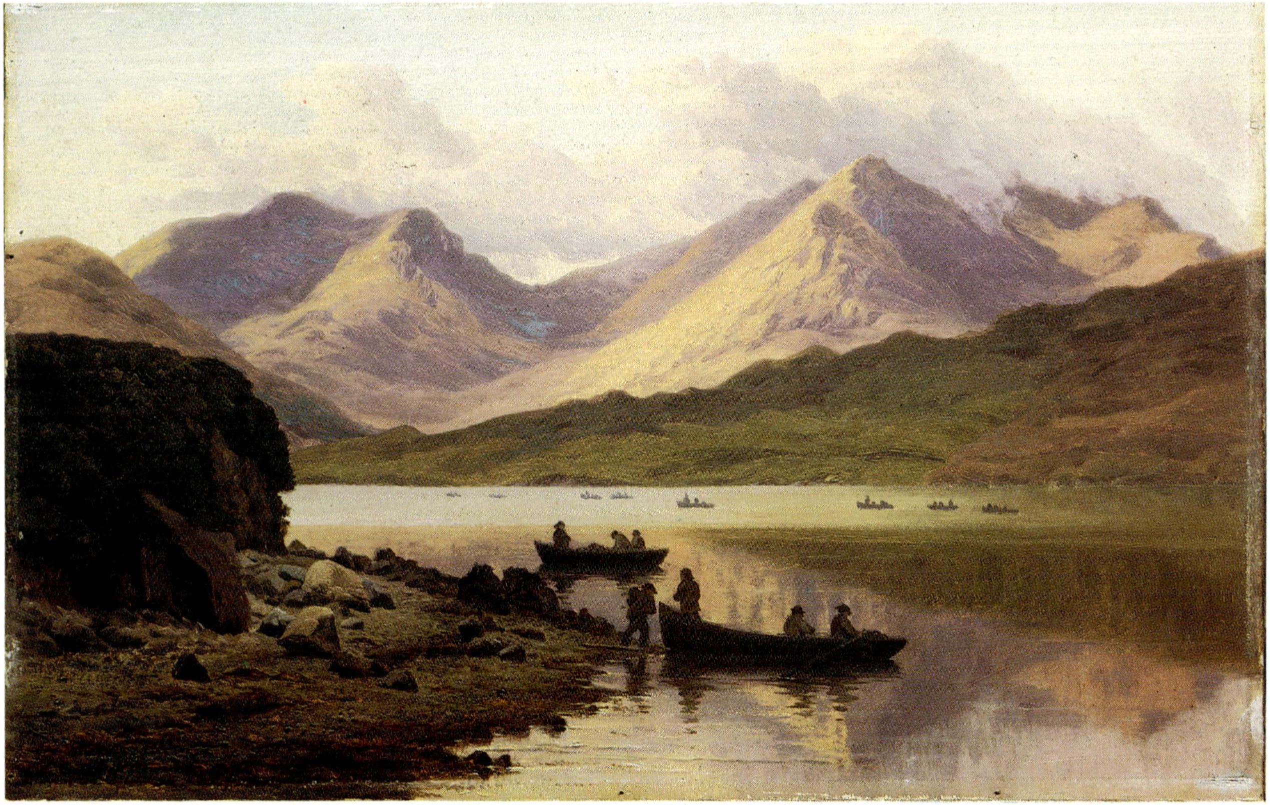

BARTHOLOMEW COLLES WATKINS, (1833-1891)

The Killaries, from Leenane, Co. Galway.

Inscribed and signed on verso:
The Killaries from Leenane/Herring Fleet putting out B. Colles Watkins RHA
Oil on canvas, 32 x 50 cms.
Bequeathed by F. Moore, 1909

Killary Harbour, on Connemara's rugged coastline, marks the county border between Galway and Mayo. The harbour is an eight-mile long fjord-like inlet surrounded by mountains. Mweelrea, the peak on the left of the painting, is the highest mountain in Connaught at two thousand six hundred and eighty-eight feet; Bengorm, the other major peak in the vicinity is on the right in this view. The lower slopes of Maumturk rise from the south shores and provide a number of vantage points from which to view the harbour. Killary, the name derived from the Irish, caolshaile-ruadh, meaning the reddish narrow sea-inlet, is the drowned lower valley of the Errif river. Beside the mouth of the harbour is another smaller inlet known as Little Killary Harbour.

The Killaries suffered from the worst ravages of the famine. Travellers to the area in the mid-19th century recall seeing people 'literally starving' although, even at that time, the clean sheltered water of the harbour was a celebrated fishing spot for visitors. Lord Sligo's fishing lodge at the foot of Mweelrea was the centre of a great deal of activity. Also at the foot of the mountain is the site of an old famine village; the remains of potato ridges, the so-called 'lazy-beds', can still be seen there.

Bartholomew C. Watkins was a Dublin born landscape painter who devoted himself to the portrayal of Irish mountain scenery particularly around Connemara, Killarney and other parts of Kerry. He took an active part in the affairs of the Royal Hibernian Academy and was popular among his fellow artists. He died while on a sketching tour in Kerry. His view of Killary Harbour is one of his two paintings of Connemara mountain scenes in the National Gallery Collection.

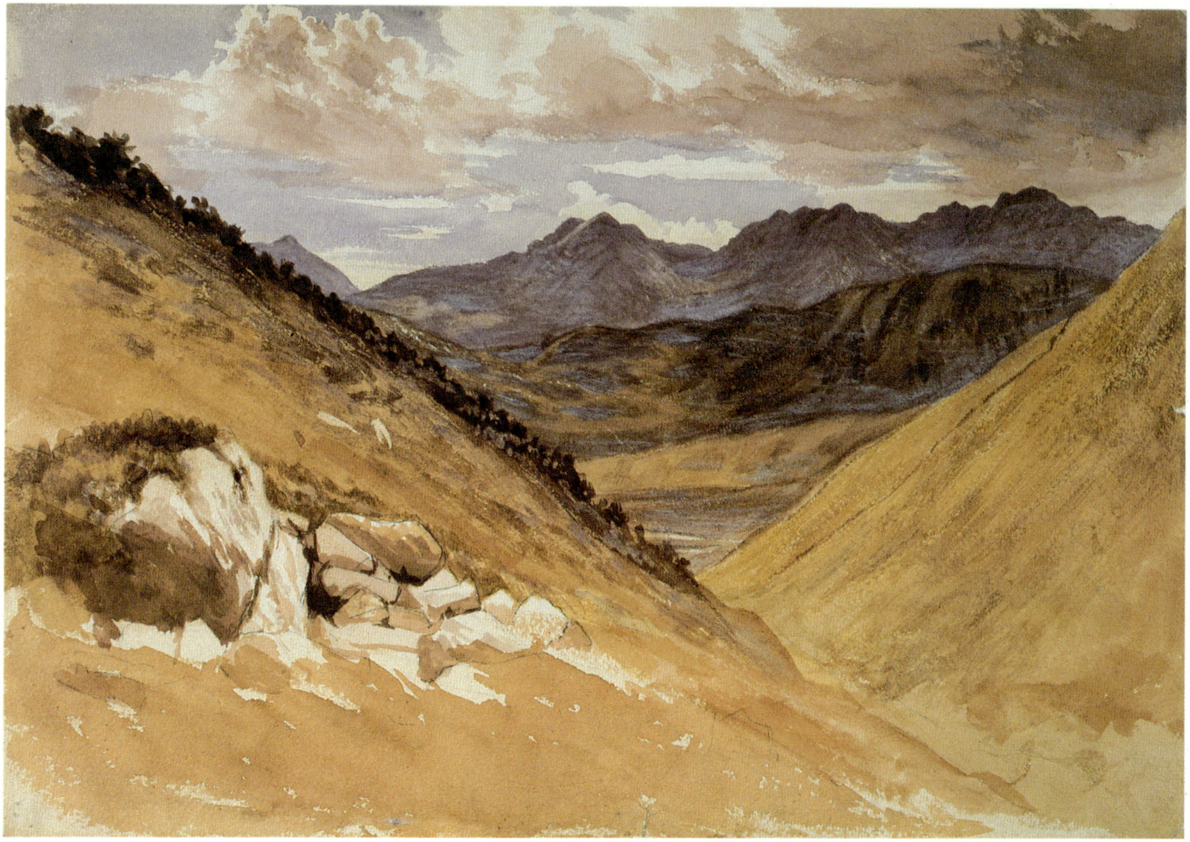

FREDERICK WILLIAM BURTON, (1816-1900).

Achill Island from Curraun Peninsula, Co. Mayo.

Pencil and watercolour on paper, 25.8 x 36.5 cms.
Bequeathed by Miss A. Callwell, 1904

Achill Island, Co. Mayo, is attached to Curraun Peninsula and the mainland by means of a narrow bridge across Achill Sound. The island is famed for its beaches and dramatic mountain and cliff scenery along the Atlantic Drive. Clare Island, Inishturk, Inishbofin and parts of Galway can be seen from there. The highest of the mountains is Slievemore and near the summit of Croaghaun, the second highest, is a two thousand one hundred and ninety one foot drop to the Atlantic Ocean.

Near the village of Doogart on the north side of the island was a missionary settlement in the 1830s headed by the Rev. E. Nangle, set up for the purpose of 'converting Romanists'. The Halls have much to say about this settlement in their work, *'Ireland: Its Scenery, Character etc.'* It seems that a considerable portion of the island belonged to the mission which was funded by subscriptions, but it was not a success. The buildings in the village of Slievemore were used as summer homes until the 1930's, but are now deserted.

Sir Frederick William Burton was born at Corofin House, Co. Clare, on April 8th 1816. His father, Samuel Frederick Burton, was a landscape artist. Burton received elementary instructions in drawing from the Brocas brothers in Dublin and he was a friend of George Petrie. He became an associate of the Royal Hibernian Academy in 1837 and an academician in 1839. He never painted in oils. He was Director of the National Gallery in London for twenty years. He was knighted in 1884 and died in Kensington on March 16th 1900.

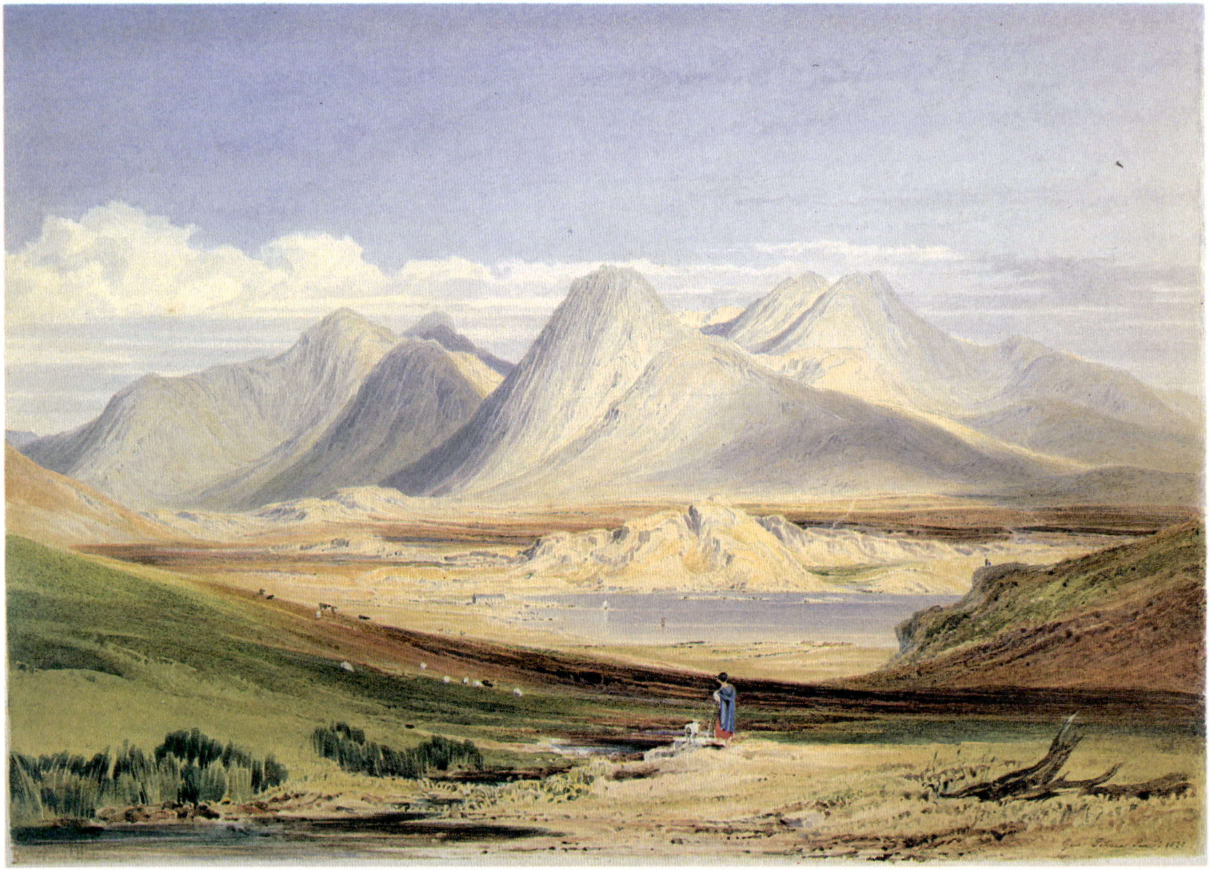

GEORGE PETRIE, (1789-1866)

The Twelve Pins, Connemara, Co. Galway from the Head of Ballinakill Bay.

Signed: Geo: Petrie Pinx^{it}. 1831
Pencil and watercolour plus varnish on paper, 29.4 x 41.1 cms.
Bequeathed by Miss A. Callwell, 1904

The Twelve Pins, or Benna Beola, are popularly known as the Twelve Bens. Situated in the heart of Connemara in western Galway, the Bens form a prominent landmark in the boggy countryside, the shape of which changes dramatically according to the angle from which it is being viewed. Petrie chose to paint the Bens from the north, focusing on the scree-bound summit of Ben Baun in the centre of this watercolour.

The combination of heather, bog and rock surfaces on the Twelve Bens provide a variety of walks and climbs for both casual and experienced mountaineers, as well as some splendid scenery for tourists. The rock climbs on Ben Corr (the peak of the conical hill), the higher mountain on the left of this view, are some of the longest climbs in Ireland. Ben Breen (peak of the hostel), the double summit to the right of Ben Baun, is rocky and steep but accessible to the less experienced hill-walker. Ben Baun (white mountain) is the highest of the Bens and from it the ridges, which give the range such an attractive outline, radiate.

This area of Ireland was only gradually being discovered by the tourist at the time Petrie painted this view in 1831. The roads and bridges which made Connemara accessible had been laid in recent years under the direction of the engineer Alexander Nimmo; they are still an essential part of its infrastructure. The beauty of the Twelve Bens remains a major part in the tourist itinerary of the country.

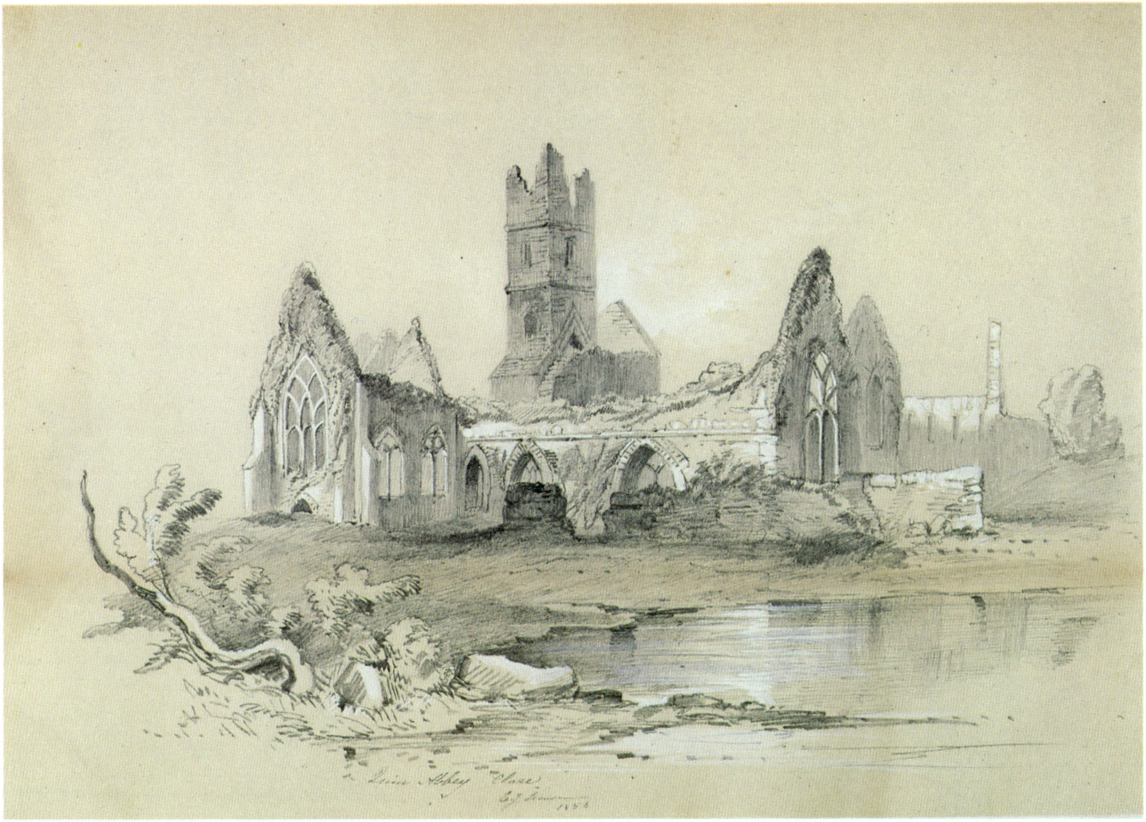

E.J. LENNOX, (19th century)

Quin Abbey, Co. Clare.

Signed: E.J. Lennox 1856.
Gouache and pencil on card, 33.2 x 43.4 cms.
Provenance unknown

The Franciscan Abbey of Quin, is unique among friaries in that it was built within the walls of a ruined Anglo-Norman castle. About 1280 Thomas de Clare built a strong symmetrical fortress with massive rounded towers at each corner on the site of a burned-out church; shortly afterwards it was ransacked by his Irish neighbours. Documentation concerning its reconstruction as an Abbey is scant and precise dating is not possible but it is likely to have been built following a licence granted to Mac-Con MacNamara by the Pope in 1433 to found an Abbey for Franciscans.

The Franciscans had arrived in Ireland in the early 13th century. During the next two centuries the friars became actively involved in the affairs of the people, and their popularity greatly increased. However pressure from the secular clergy encouraged an element among them to return to the strict observance of the rule of St. Francis; it is thought that Quin Abbey was one of the early such 'Observantine' houses in Ireland.

MacNamara chose to adapt the ruin for his new Abbey with much of the old castle providing the building material. Window reveals splaying inward and outward were inserted in the nine and a half foot thick south wall, the east wall was remodelled, and the north and west walls were used as foundations for claustral buildings; a transcept was added on the south side. The slender belfry was unusually tall, rising to a height of ninety feet. The claustral buildings, not visible in this view, are in a remarkable state of preservation and among the best examples of their kind in the country. The Abbey remained in use until the late 18th century. It is now protected as a National Monument. Little is known about the artist, E.J. Lennox; this mid-19th century view of Quin Abbey is the only work by him in the National Gallery Collection.

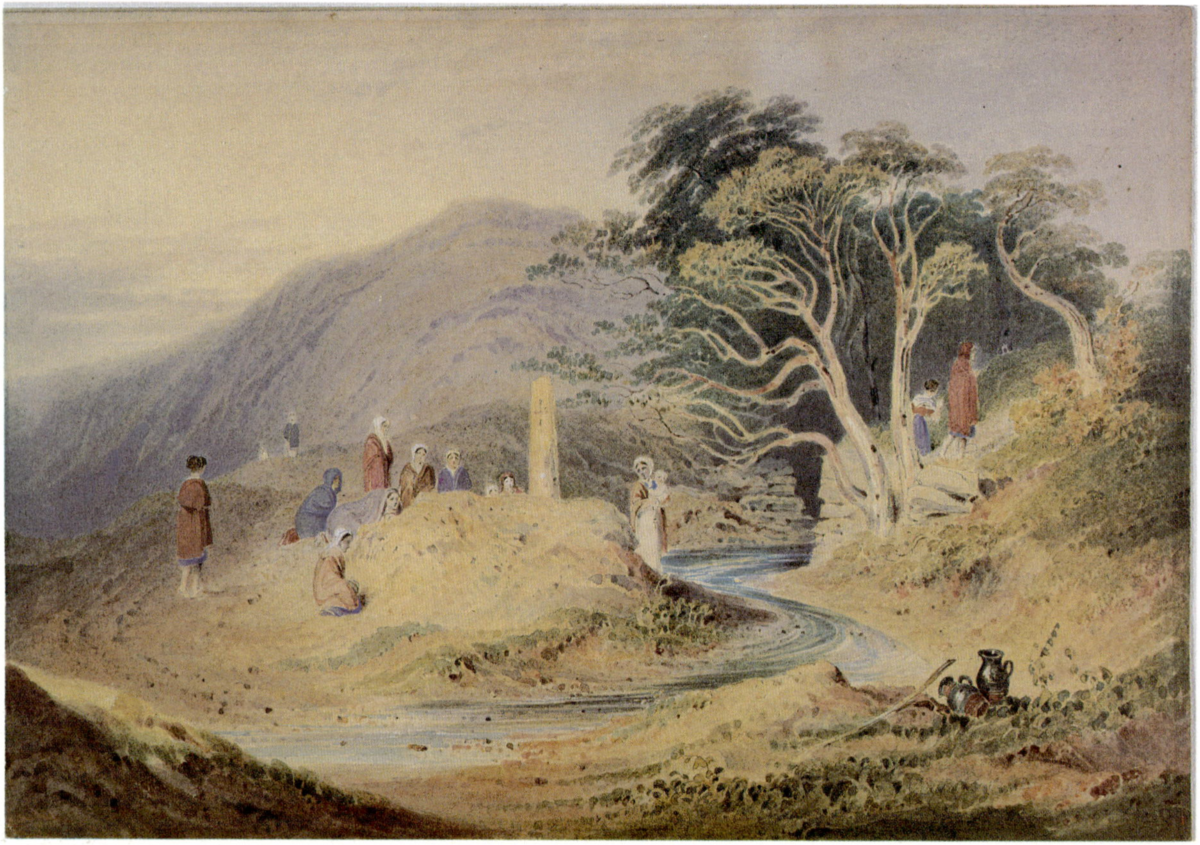

GEORGE PETRIE, (1789-1866)

Pilgrims at St. Brigid's Well, Liscannor, Co. Clare.

Watercolour on paper, 18.5 x 26 cms.
Bequeathed by Miss M. Stokes, 1900

George Petrie chose St. Brigid's Well in Liscannor to illustrate the ancient custom of pilgrimage to a holy well in Ireland. There were thousands of holy wells around the country, often springs of clear water which were seldom used for domestic purposes. They were usually named after an early Christian saint who had preached in the area. On 'patron day', (pronounced 'pattern'), hundreds of pilgrims would journey to the well believing in its power to cure disease.

The tradition associated with each well differed. The most common form of ritual performed on 'patron day' was the 'making of the rounds', walking clockwise around the well a number of times reciting certain prayers and perhaps kneeling between each 'round'. Pilgrims unable or unwilling to carry out the sometimes painful ritual could pay someone to do it by proxy. It was believed that the desired cure would be effected if one followed the ritual as prescribed, and with good intentions; if, however, one wanted to lay a curse on a neighbour one walked anti-clockwise around the well, with evil intentions.

The annual 'patron day' was a very popular practice but it would seem that the festivity of the occasion somewhat supplanted the piety, and the events were suppressed by the Roman Catholic clergy in the 19th century. 'Patron day' to St. Brigid's Well was the Saturday preceeding the last Sunday of July, when crowds from the Aran Islands as well as from the mainland assembled to sing throughout the night and then to proceed to Lahinch to continue the pilgrimage. However Petrie chose to overlook the more raucous aspect of the holy well, presenting a quiet scene of piety and faith surrounding one of Co. Clare's holy wells.

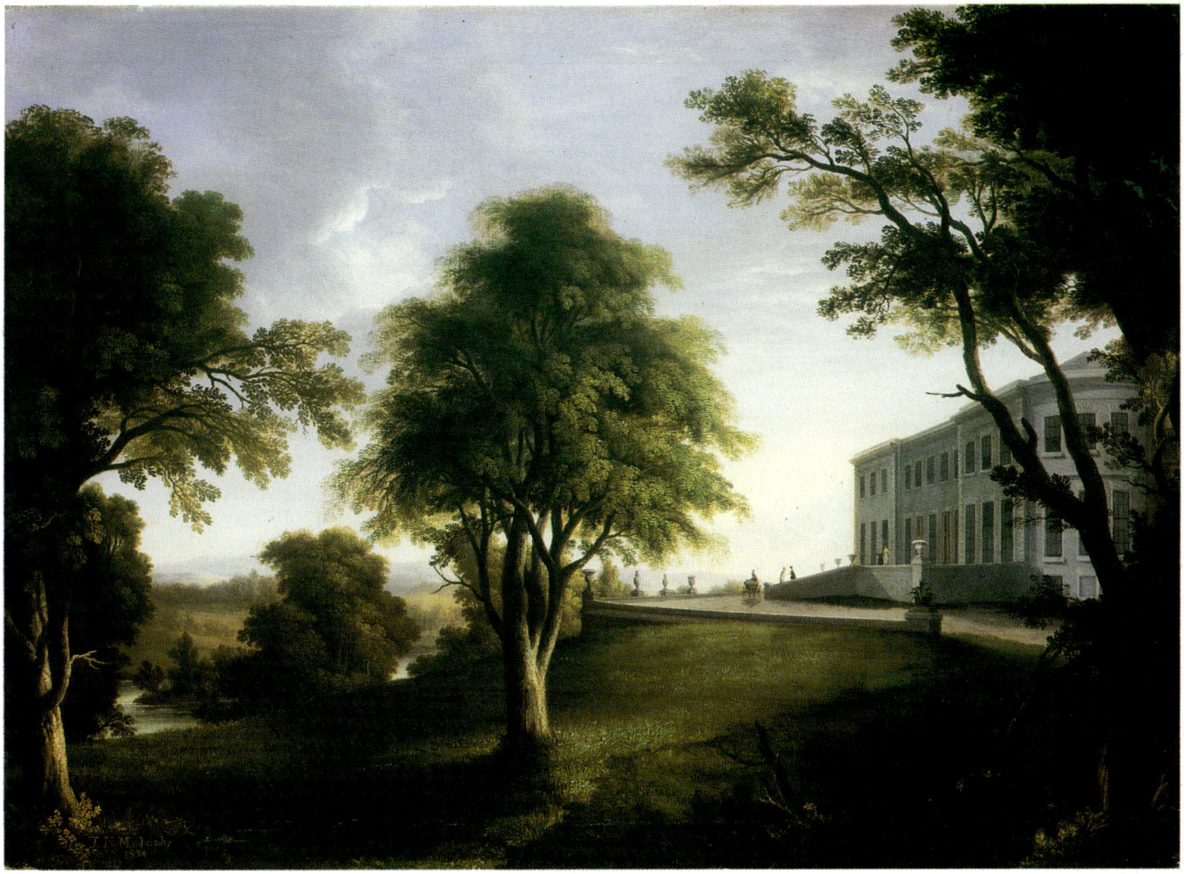

JEREMIAH MULCAHY,
(fl. c.1830-1889).

Curragh Chase House, Co. Limerick.

Signed and dated: J.H. Mulcahy 1834.
Oil on canvas, 56 x 75.5 cms.
Purchased, 1966

The beautiful setting of Curragh Chase House, near Adare, is the most attractive feature of this 18th century classical building. The landscape was largely created by Sir Aubrey de Vere in the early 19th century. His son, Aubrey, the noted Victorian poet and author, eloquently described his father's love of landscape gardening when he recorded that it was his 'one mode of taking out the poetry which was so deeply seated within him.'

Nevertheless the house is perhaps best known as the home of the younger Aubrey de Vere. He was born there in 1814 and, having spent some years travelling, he returned in 1854. He lived quietly, corresponding with his numerous friends and entertaining visitors. He died in 1902 in the small bedroom he had occupied as a child. In 1941 the house was gutted by fire; de Vere's archive, known to have contained manuscripts of Sir Alfred Tennyson and of William Wordsworth as well as a lengthy correspondence with Cardinal Newman, was lost in the blaze. The house was never restored but the property was acquired by the Government and the fine grounds are now maintained as a public parkland.

Jeremiah Hodges Mulcahy was a native of Limerick; for about thirty years he made a living chiefly by painting the estates of the landowners of Limerick and Clare. He also worked as a topographical draughtsman for engravers which included a series of views for Halls *'Ireland: Its Scenery, Character, etc.'* In 1842 he opened a school of painting in Limerick which continued until he moved to Dublin in 1862.

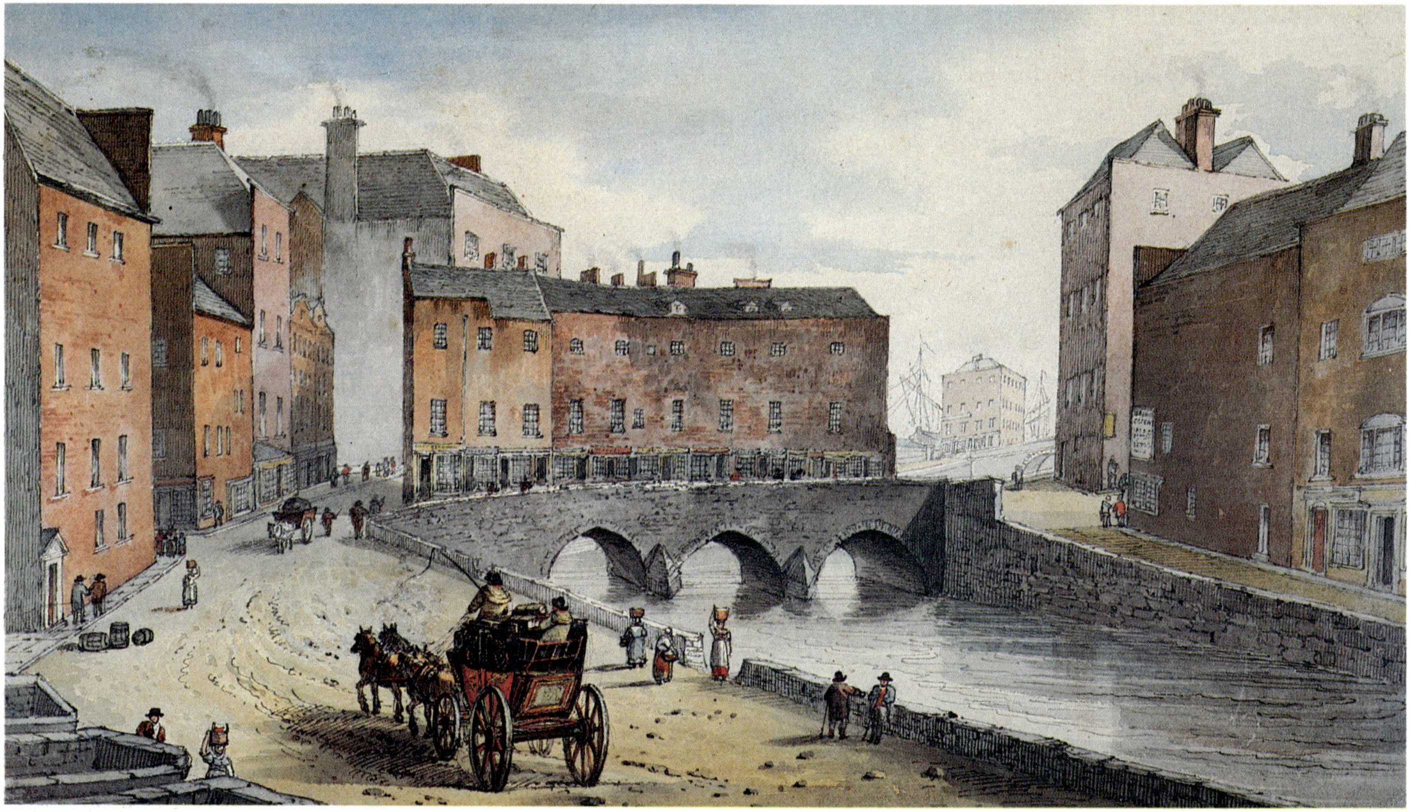

JAMES HENRY BROCAS,
(1790-1846)

Old Baal's Bridge, Limerick.

Ink and watercolour on paper, 23.3 x 39.5 cms.
Purchased, 1904

Old Baal's Bridge spanned the Abbey river, a tributary of the Shannon. Situated in the historic part of Limerick city it linked the land known as English Town on the northern bank with Irish Town on the southern bank. Unlike most bridges in Ireland, Baal's bridge was private property and consequently its owner could build on it. In the 17th century it supported a row of houses and shops on either side with a rather narrow passage between them. In 1761 its owner, Viscount Shannon, agreed to sell the row on the east side to the Government; the buildings were pulled down and the roadway widened.

In 1775 the bridge was damaged when an unusually high spring tide swept part of it down river and several houses collapsed; they were repaired and remained in use until the entire bridge, which had four arches, not three as the drawing suggests, was demolished and a new one put in its place. Renamed Ball's Bridge, it was opened in 1831 and now connects Broad Street with Mary Street.

James Henry Brocas was the eldest son of Henry Brocas, a landscape artist. Three of his brothers also trained as artists and, as a family, they were renowned for their views of Dublin; engravings both by and after one or other of them appeared regularly in the guidebooks and periodicals of the time. James, however, had little to do with this reputation: most of his topographical work recorded scenery in Munster. He settled in Cork in 1834 where he died twelve years later.

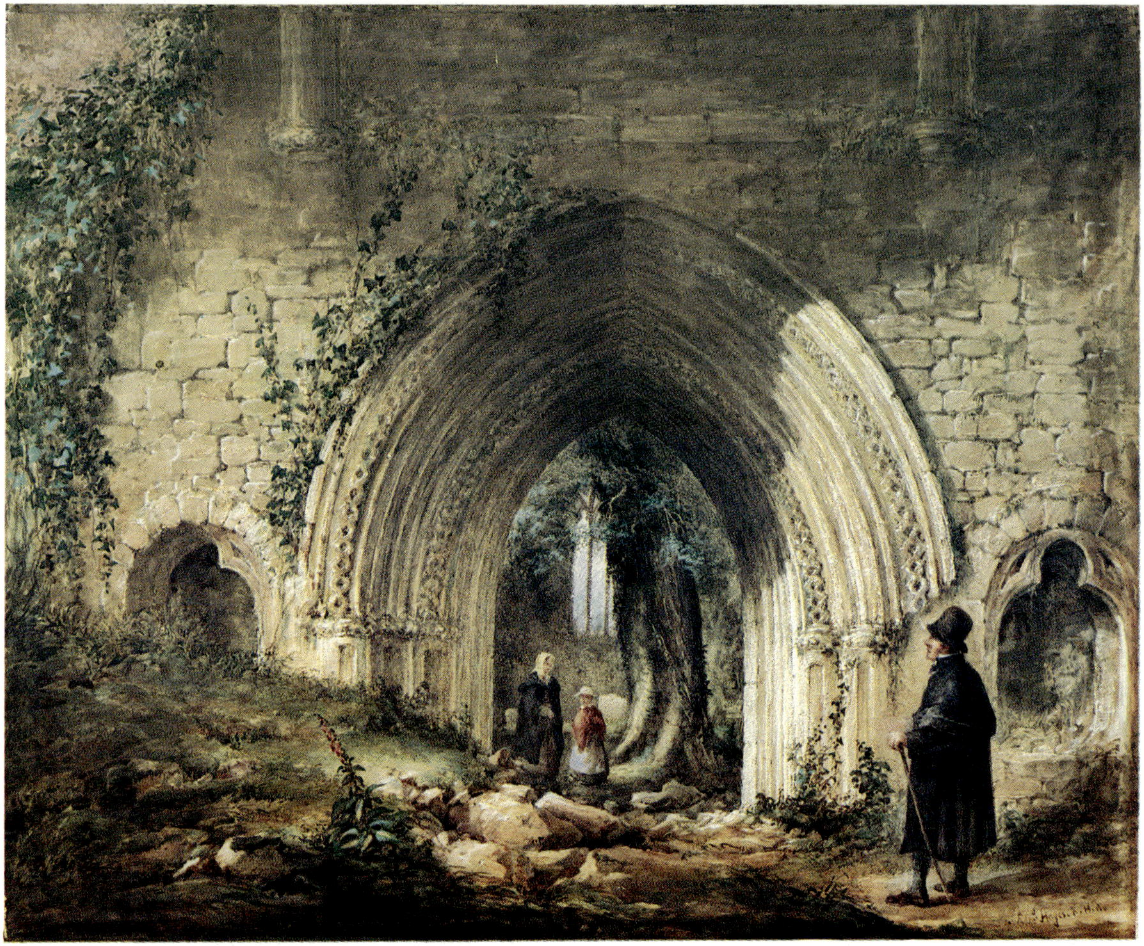

EDWARD HAYES, (1797-1864)

The Choir Doorway, Athassel Priory, Co. Tipperary.

Signed: Edwd. Hayes R.H.A.
Watercolour on paper, 46.4 x 56 cms.
Presented, Miss Geoghegan, 1923

Edward Hayes was born in Co. Tipperary. He exhibited frequently in the Royal Hibernian Academy, the main body of his work consisted of miniatures and small portraits in pencil and watercolour although he occasionally exhibited landscapes.

This delicate watercolour of the choir doorway in St. Edmund's Priory depicts one of the finest features of this extensive Augustinian monastery on the west bank of the river Suir. The ruins of the priory cover nearly four acres surrounded by a high wall with the entrance through a portcullis gateway. A small town grew up outside the walls. It was razed in 1330 and subsequently vanished.

The Priory is said to have been founded by William FitzAdelm de Burgo. He died in 1205 but his descendants continued to support the Canons. The widely splayed west doorway of the choir is depicted from the nave in this view; above it is a shallow arched recess which possibly held the great crucifix or rood. The extensive claustral buildings are to the south of the church. Much of the Priory was destroyed in 1447, and although some additions were made since then the nave was left roofless. It is now a National Monument.

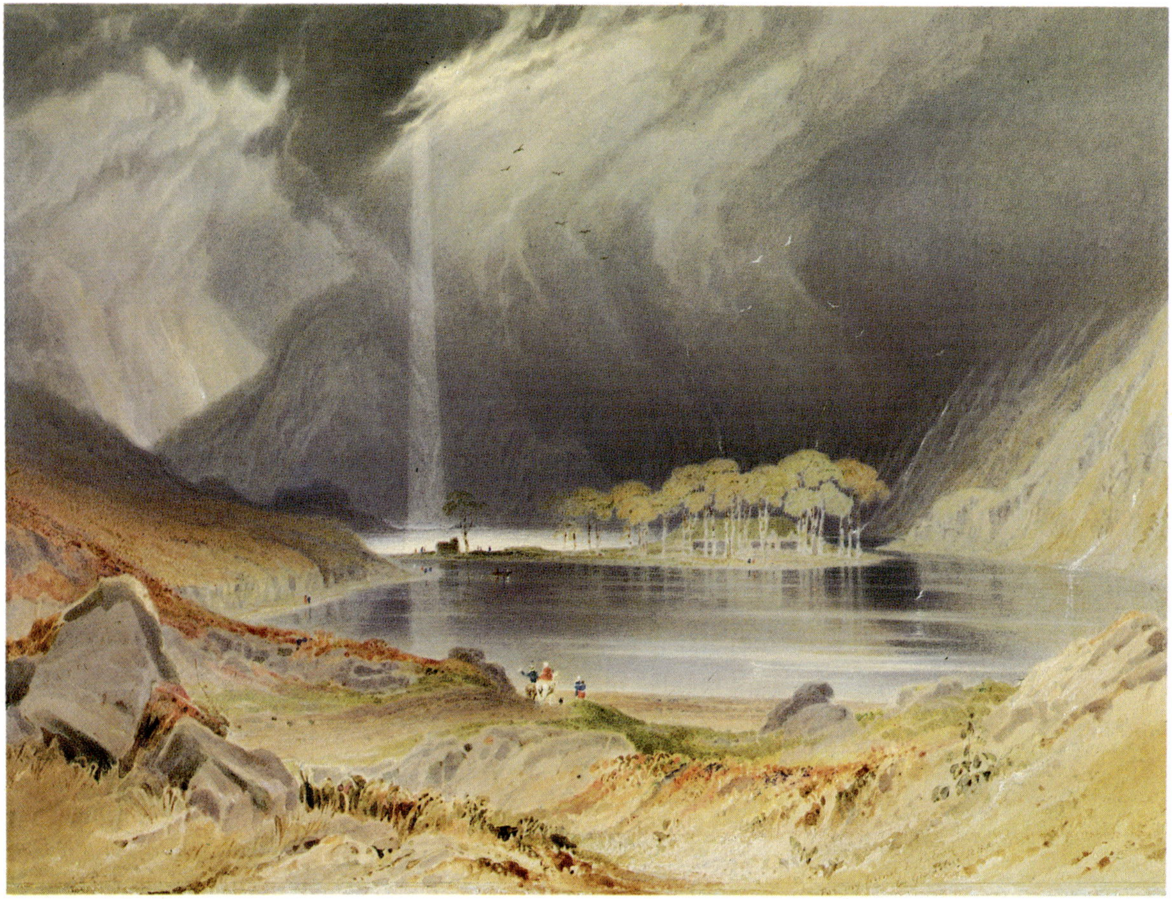

GEORGE PETRIE, (1789-1866)

Gougane Barra Lake with the Hermitage of St. Finbarr, Co. Cork.

Inscribed and signed: To my friend R. Callwell by Geo Petrie. R.H.A.
Watercolour on paper, 30.9 x 39.7 cms.
Bequeathed, Miss A. Callwell, 1904

Gougane Barra, at the source of the river Lee, is isolated by steep rocky mountains. It is closely associated with the 7th century Irish monk, St. Finbarr, who established his first settlement on a small island in the lake.

The ruins of what are reputed to be the saint's original cell and part of the first chapel on the island have long been a place of pilgrimage. Despite the difficult terrain on the access routes to Gougane Barra thousands of pilgrims flocked there when it was widely believed that the water had the power to cure all diseases in both animal and man. A small oratory was erected on the island which is connected to the shore by a narrow causeway. During the 19th century the festivities of the annual 'patron Day' were discouraged by the clergy.

The reaction of visitors to Gougane Barra differed widely. Petrie, obviously captivated by the extraordinary beauty of the lonely spot, heightened the spiritual aura of the lake with a strong shaft of light breaking through dark rolling clouds. Brewer, a contemporary of the artist, was not quite so impressed. In his *Beauties of Ireland* he maintained that such solemn places nurtured a 'gloomy and ascetic view of religious aspirations' compared with the 'brighter and more philosophic complexion in countries uniformly favourable to the bustle of commerce', Gougane Barra remains a popular detour for tourists on the road to Bantry from Bandon.

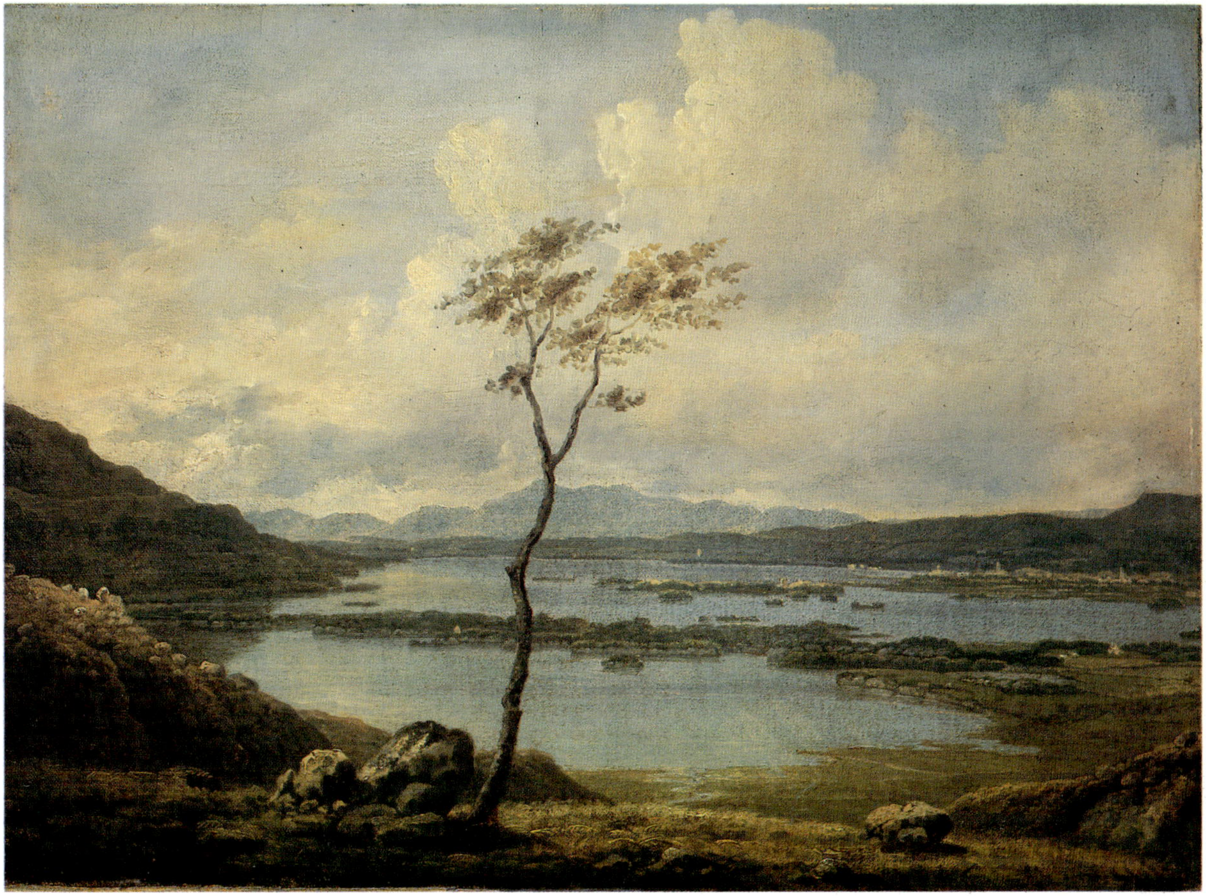

JONATHAN FISHER, (fl.1763-1809)

The Lower Lake, Killarney.

Oil on canvas, 39.8 x 52 cms.
Purchased, 1966

The Lakes of Killarney, Co. Kerry, lie at the foot of the Macgillycuddy Reeks and the Mangerton Mountains. There are three lakes; the Upper Lake, Muckross or the Middle Lake and Lough Leane or the Lower Lake. They are separated from each other by narrow channels: the Meeting of the Waters between Lough Leane and Muckross Lake, and the Long Range between the latter and the Upper Lake. Lough Leane is closest to Killarney.

The Lakes are formed and supplied by small lakes and streamlets and the only outlet is the river Laune which flows from Lough Leane into Dingle Bay. One of the small tributaries is the Owengarriff river which flows down from Torc mountain, into Muckross Lake as Torc Waterfall, fifty eight feet high. After the bog 'moved' in Sliabh Luacra near the Cork border on 28th December 1896 and swept away a house, killing eight people, household furniture was found in the lakes fifteen miles away. Many of the famous views of the Ring of Kerry are to be seen near the lakes: such as Ladies' View, which is reputed to have derived its name from the delight of Queen Victoria's Ladies-in-Waiting on a visit to the area.

Jonathan Fisher was a self-taught artist born in Dublin. He was originally a woollen-draper in the Liberties. From 1778 until his death in 1809 he was Supervisor of Stamps in the Stamp Office in George's Lane.

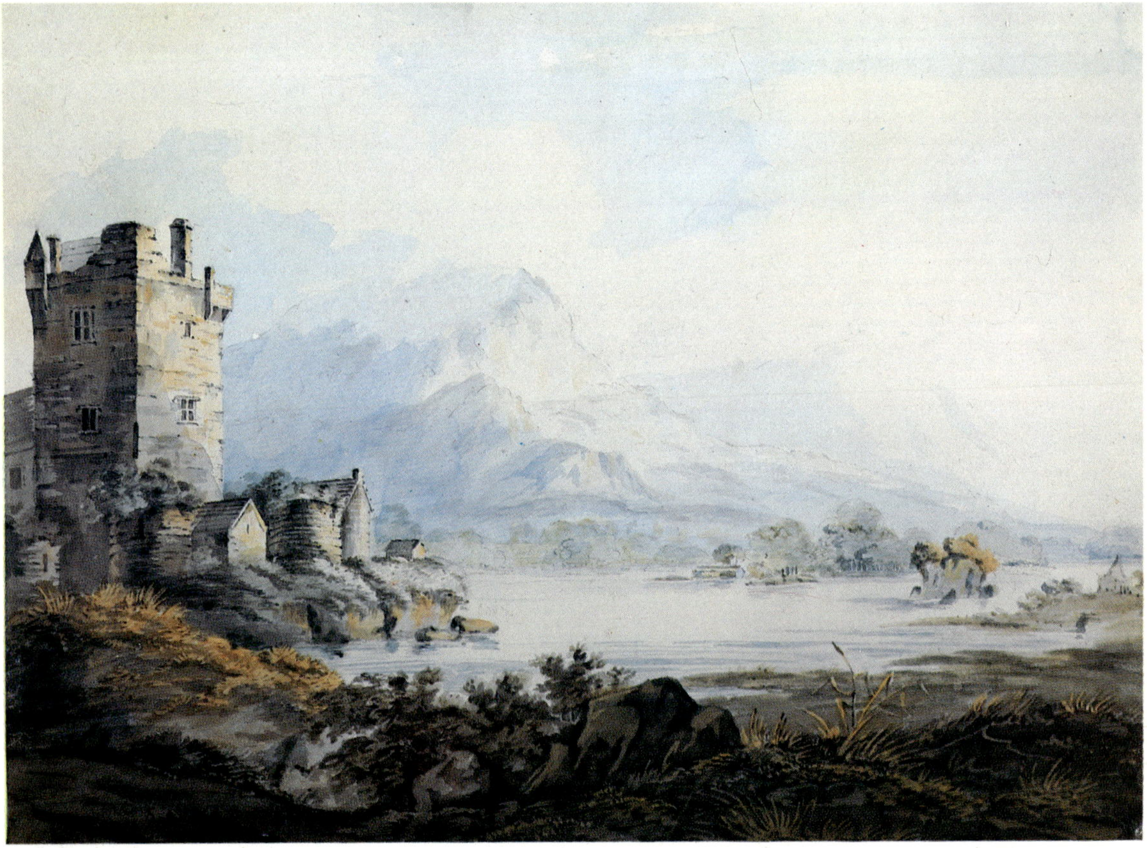

REDMOND BARRY,
(18th-19th century)

Ross Castle, Lough Leane, Co. Kerry.

Signed on verso: Redmond Barry Pinxit 1800.
Watercolour on paper, 40.5 x 54 cms.
Purchased, 1969

The composition of Redmond Barry's watercolour emphasises the prominence of Ross Castle on the Lower Lake of Killarney. The remains of this once important fortress comprise a massive 15th century tower house with a small bawn and some later additions. It was the seat of the O'Donoghue Mór and was probably erected by one of the early chieftains of the clan.

There are numerous legends connected with the castle in association with the name of O'Donoghue. The best known of these concerns a chieftain who is believed to have leapt out of a window into the lake followed by his horse, library and table. According to the legend his possessions turned into stone and may be seen rising above the water, and the O'Donoghue chief appears once a year gliding across the lake on a large white horse.

Superstition associated with the castle may have had a more serious side-effect. In 1652, when most of the country had succumbed to Cromwell's Parliamentary troops, Ross Castle was one of the last strongholds under Irish control. It would seem that it was well prepared for a lengthy siege. However General Ludlow, then in command of the English forces, designed an offensive which, perhaps unwittingly, fulfilled the ancient prophecy that 'Ross may all assault disdain, till on Loch Lein strange ships shall sail' for when Ludlow launched a number of boats in an attempt to attack from both land and water, the Irish garrison surrendered without a fight. This was the last major incident at Ross Castle; from then it gradually fell into decay. This view is the only work by the artist in the National Gallery of Ireland.

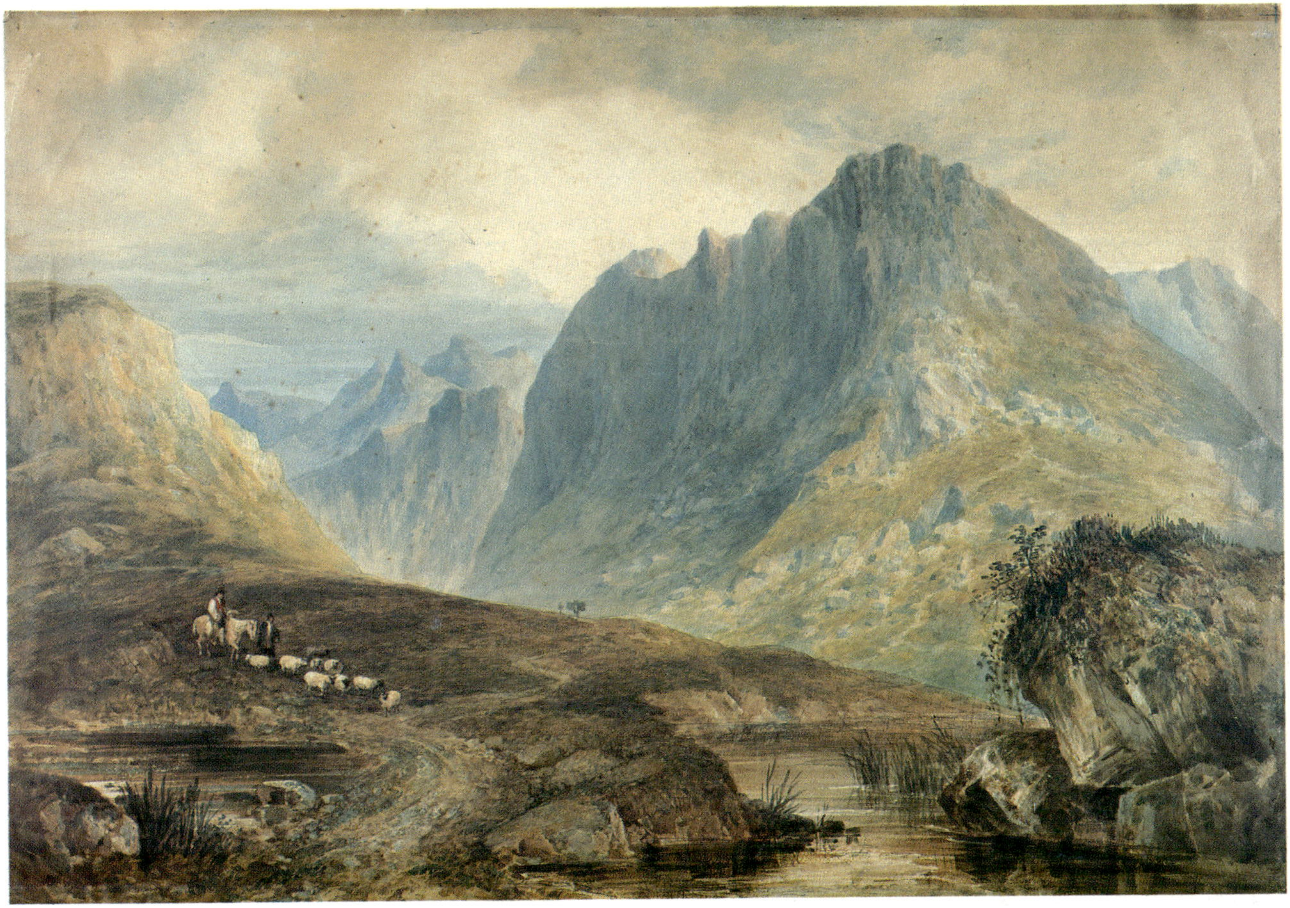

HENRY BROCAS SENIOR,
(1768-1838)

The Gap of Dunloe, Killarney, Co. Kerry.

Pencil and watercolour on paper, 55 x 78 cms.
Transferred from the National Museum, 1966

The Gap of Dunloe is about four miles south west of Killarney in Co. Kerry and is one of the most celebrated of Ireland's tourist spots. 'The principal feature of the pass is the height of the rocks which bound it compared with the narrow track of road and the insignificant streamlet which courses through it'. (Black's *Guide to Ireland,* 1912). The gorge itself is approximately four miles long, lying between Carrantuohill, the highest peak in Ireland at three thousand four hundred and fourteen feet in height, in the Macgillycuddy Reeks and the Tomies and Purple Mountains, at two thousand four hundred and thirteen and two thousand, seven hundred and thirty nine feet high respectively. The river Loe runs along the defile, joining the river Laune which flows into Dingle Bay with the Lakes of Killarney. There are three small lakes along the length of the Gap: Black Lake, Cushvalley Lake and Auger Lake.

Kate Kearney's Cottage, named after a local beauty in the early 1800s who sold goats' milk laced with poteen to the tourists, is now a souvenir shop where ponies can also be hired to bring present-day tourists to the spot where boats embark on a trip around the Lakes through the Meeting of the Waters, another beauty spot.

Henry Brocas Senior was born in Dublin in 1766, the fifth son of Robert Brocas and his wife Bridget (née Taylor). His brother was James Brocas (1754-1780) the portraitist. Henry Brocas was a landscape painter and a prolific engraver. He died in 1838.

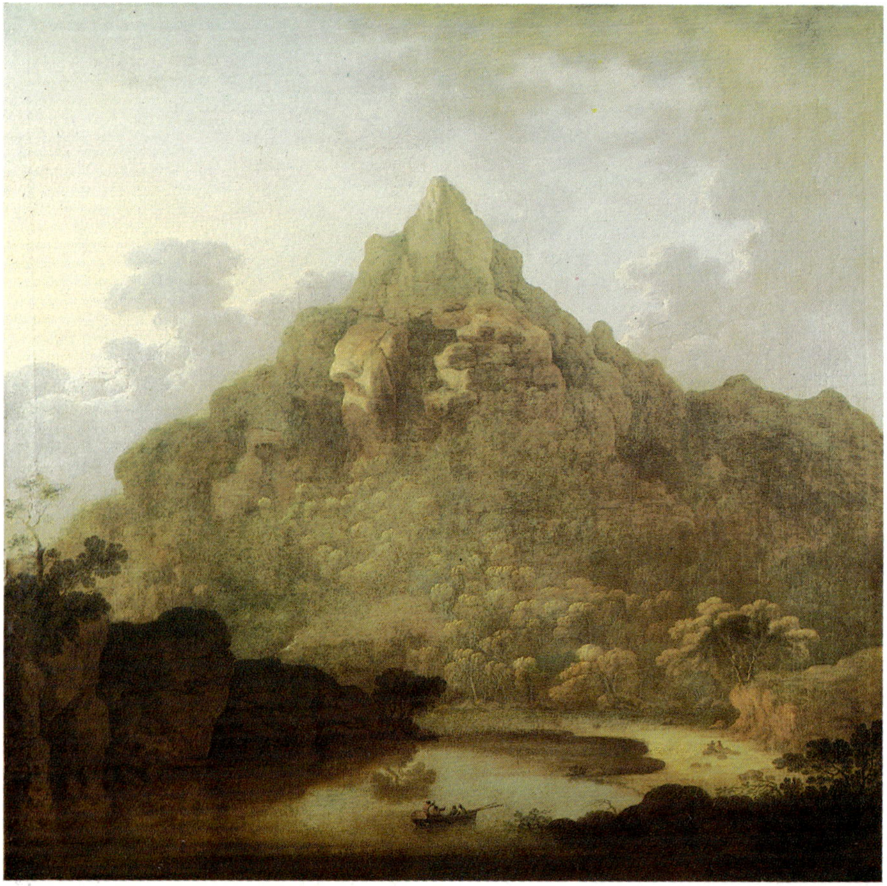

JONATHAN FISHER, (fl.1763-1809)

The Eagle's Nest, Killarney, Co. Kerry.

Oil on canvas, 117 x 117 cms.
Purchased, 1967

Fisher's painting of the Eagle's Nest in Killarney, Co. Kerry, captures the dramatic outline of the rock which dominates the channel of the upper and middle lakes. On a promontory opposite an almost perpendicular cliff two men can be seen beside a smoking cannon. Firing a cannon was the method of demonstrating the remarkable echoes of Eagle's Nest which attracted the attention of tourists in the 18th and 19th century. One tourist handbook, published in 1852, described the effect: 'The report produced a discordant crash, as if the whole pile of rocks were rent asunder, and the succeeding echoes resemble a tremendous peal of thunder. Twelve reverberations, and sometimes more, may be distinctly counted; and, what appears extraordinary, after the sound has been totally lost, it occasionally revives, becomes louder and louder for a few seconds, and then dies away.'

The cannon was usually discharged just as a number of musicians, situated on the river banks fifty yards away from the cliff, finished playing. Arthur Young accompanied his description of the echoes of Eagle's Nest with a map showing the best position for the musicians and the point at which the echoes could be heard to the greatest effect.

Jonathan Fisher was a minor artist in the emerging school of Irish landscape painting in the 18th century. He started publishing his own engravings in 1770, and in 1795 he attempted the first comprehensive coverage of Irish scenery when he produced sixty aquatints of views from all over Ireland.

INDEX OF ARTISTS